HOW TO BE TOP

ARCTURUS

CONTENTS

CONTENTS

INTRODUCTION

Math, English and Science are a vital part of any child's learning and development. In this book we have devised a whole variety of tests and exercises that will improve their understanding and knowledge of these subjects. Divided into chapters, every important aspect of these topics is covered.

In the Math chapter we have placed particular emphasis on the core skills of addition, subtraction, multiplication and division. Also covered are fractions, areas and angles, and square and cube numbers.

The Science chapter is wide-ranging and covers many areas, including the human body, plants, electricity, light and sound.

The English chapter includes spelling, grammar, speech and reading skills. In fact, because spelling is such an integral part of the English language, we have devoted two sections to it.

We recommend that you give your child one of the tests or exercises each day. It is important for them to feel happy with each explanation before embarking on the accompanying Test and you may want to check and make sure that they have fully understood the explanation. It is a vital part of a child's development to feel that parental interest and

INTRODUCTION

support are present at every step, but it is equally important for children to realise that once a Test has started there is no "outside" help until the answers have been checked. Don't rush your child, but let them work at their own pace.

In the Math section, encourage your child to work without a calculator. Times tables have been included throughout, as has a multiplication grid for the numbers from 13 to 20.

Although there is space for many of the answers to be written in this book, we recommend that you have your child write all the answers in a separate notebook. That way, if you wish to repeat any of the tests at a later date, you will be able to compare the child's speed and accuracy.

Learning should be fun and not a chore! Practising the exercises in this book should help to ensure that your child improves significantly in these core subjects.

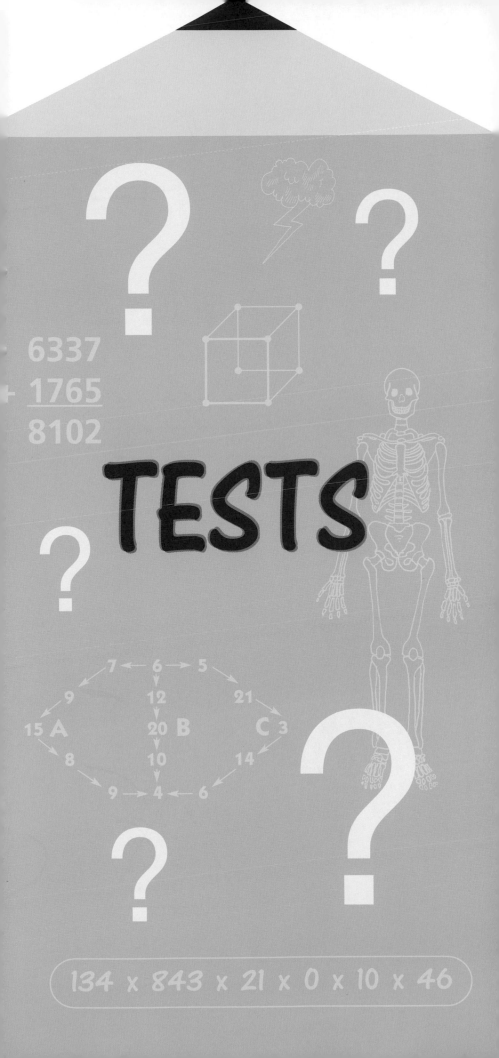

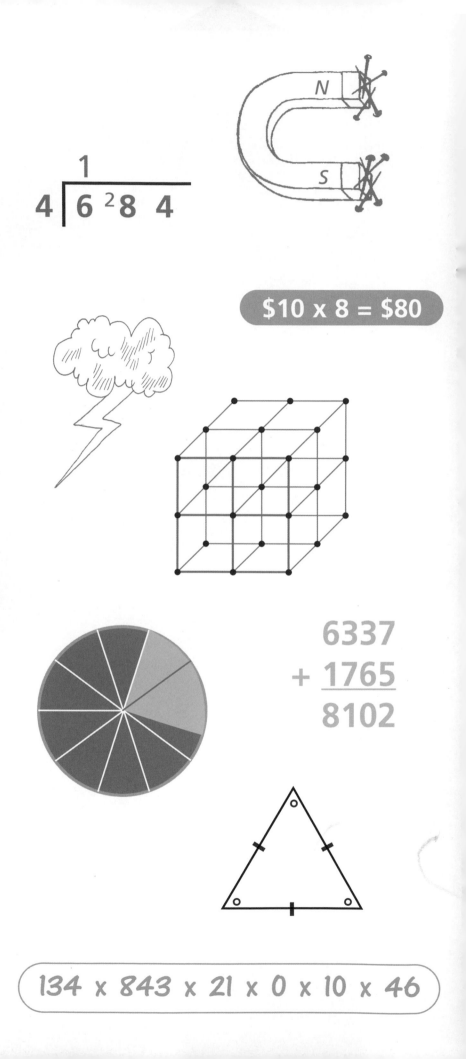

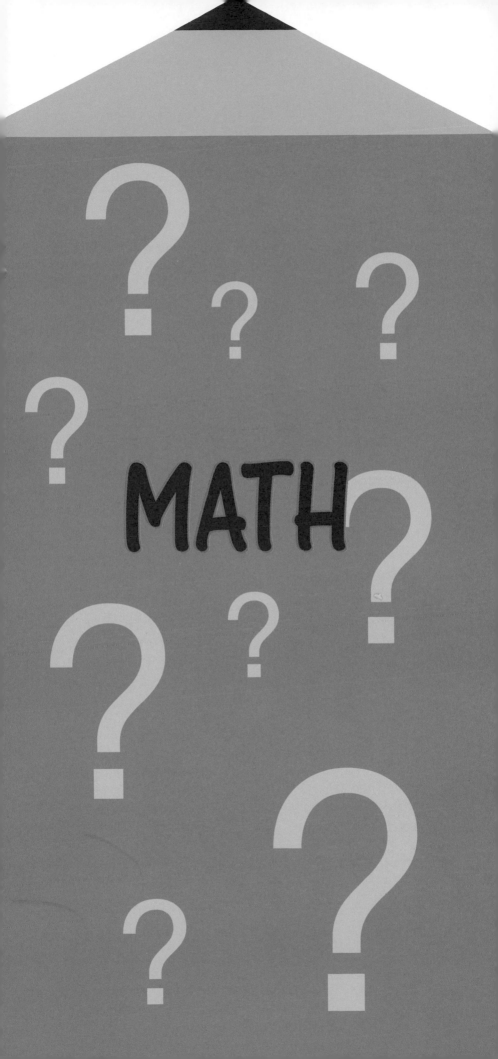

It is a wonderful fact that in Mathematics we use only **nine** figures and **zero**:

1 2 3 4 5 6 7 8 9 0

These 10 symbols make all the numbers in the universe. They can be used for counting the fingers on your hand or for telling us how many people there are in the world. In all numbers the position of each figure shows its value. You can see how the value of the figure **3** changes in this box:

THOUSANDS	HUNDREDS	TENS	UNITS	HOW TO READ THE NUMBER
			3	Three
		3	0	Thirty (three tens)
	3	0	0	Three hundred
3	0	0	0	Three thousand

Put in the right figures, with zeros where needed:

THOUSANDS	HUNDREDS	TENS	UNITS	HOW TO READ THE NUMBER
1. ___	___	___	___	Seventy
2. ___	___	___	___	Six
3. ___	___	___	___	Five thousand
4. ___	___	___	___	Eight hundred

All numbers can be **POSITIVE** or **NEGATIVE**. On a warm day a thermometer shows positive numbers, but on a very cold day it registers negative numbers because the temperature is **BELOW ZERO**. To show that a number is negative we put a **subtraction** or **minus** sign before it, as in **-5**, which we call **"minus five."**

5. Write the correct **POSITIVE** and **NEGATIVE** numbers for the dots without numbers:

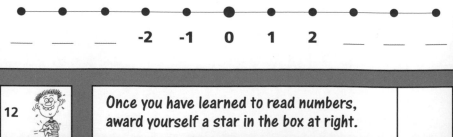

___ ___ ___ -2 -1 0 1 2 ___ ___ ___

Once you have learned to read numbers, award yourself a star in the box at right.

ADDING
TEST 2

Grandpa has to take some tablets every day. He has to take two tablets early in the morning, one tablet after lunch, and three at nighttime. How many tablets does Grandpa take each day?

If you can add up, all you have to say is, "2 plus 1 is 3, and 3 plus 3 is 6." So Grandpa takes 6 tablets every day.

Adding is easy, even when the numbers seem to get big. Always start with the **Units** column, and then move to the **Tens**. Suppose we want to add 25 and 19. We work it out like this:

	TENS	UNITS	
	2	5	Add the Units column: 5 + 9 =14. Put the 4 in the Units answer and carry the 1 (which is 1 Ten) to the Ten column. Now add 2 and 1 and the new 1 to obtain 4 for the Tens answer.
+	1	9	
	4	4	
	1		

Now try these by yourself:

1.	T	U		2.	T	U		3.	T	U
	1	4			1	7			2	8
+	1	1		+	1	5		+	1	4

4. Amanda has 3 red pencils, 2 blue ones, and 4 green ones. How many pencils is that? _____

5. Jimmy has 2 computer games. He buys 2 more with his allowance and is given 5 more for his birthday. How many does he now have altogether? _____

6. How many legs do two people and two spiders have altogether? (Remember: each spider has 8 legs!) _____

Now that you have completed this page, award yourself a star in the box at left.

13

Even if you are adding hundreds together, it's easy. Start with the **Units** column, move to the **Tens**, and finish with the **Hundreds**. If your total for any column is bigger than 9, remember to write the second figure in this column, but carry the first figure to the next column on the left. See if you can follow what happens when we want to add 187 to 154. Here we go!

	H	T	U
	1	8	7
+	1	5	4
	3	4	1
	1	1	

Can you see that the Units total 11? The Tens total 14, which includes the carry-over figure from the 11. And the Hundreds total 3 (1 +1 + the carry-over 1).

Try the first 5 questions in the same way.
Then put on your thinking cap for some harder problems!

1.

H	T	U
2	5	4
+ 1	7	7

2.

H	T	U
3	6	8
+ 2	5	4

3.

H	T	U
1	0	5
+ 2	5	9

4.

H	T	U
4	7	3
+ 2	9	9

5.

H	T	U
3	4	9
+ 2	6	8

6. Joe does 20 problems in one lesson, 30 in the next lesson, and 25 in the third lesson. How many problems does Joe do altogether in the 3 lessons? _____

7. In 2007 Mr. Jenkins picked 117 apples from his tree, and in 2008 he picked 138 apples. How many apples did he pick in the two years? _____

8. The Thompson family took a summer camping holiday that cost $475 and a short autumn break that cost $228. What was the total cost of their two holidays? _____

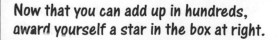

14   Now that you can add up in hundreds, award yourself a star in the box at right.

Are we ready to go into Thousands? If you know how to deal with **Hundreds, Tens,** and **Units,** it's easy, because you simply continue in the same way. Suppose you want to add 2567 and 1708. **First, put the figures in the correct columns:**

Th	H	T	U
2	5	6	7
+ 1	7	0	8
4	2	7	5
1		1	

Add the Units, to get 15. Put the 5 in the Units answer and carry the 1 to the Tens column. Add the Tens, to get 7. Add the Hundreds, to get 12. Put the 2 in the Hundreds answer, and carry the 1 to the Thousands column, to make 4 Thousand.

Here are three questions like this, and then some more problems!

1.

Th	H	T	U
	1	1	8	6
+	1	0	9	5

2.

Th	H	T	U
	2	7	4	4
+	1	8	3	7

3.

Th	H	T	U
	3	9	0	8
+	2	7	6	5

4. Tonio sold 1028 ice cream cones on Saturday and 1054 on Sunday. How many cones did he sell that weekend? _____

5. Mrs. Honiton paid $1599 for new living room furniture, $727 for new carpets, and $1614 for some cupboards and countertops. What was her total expenditure? _____

6. Mr. Lambert earned $1428 in January, $1297 in February, and $1985 in March. How much did he earn altogether in those 3 months? _____

Once you have completed this page, award yourself a star in the box at left.

15

Mom leaves 5 cupcakes on a plate in the kitchen. When she comes back from the phone there are only 4 cupcakes on the plate. 1 cupcake has been taken away! 5 take away 1 is 4. Taking away and subtracting are the same. So we can say, "Subtract 1 from 5 and you get 4." We can also use the minus sign and say, "5 - 1 is 4." The equals sign is very useful too, because we can now write **5 - 1 = 4**.

Jenny has 8 candies. She gives 3 away. How many does she now have?
Yes, she now has 5. To find the answer you can start with 8 and count backwards 3 steps: **8, 7, 6, 5**. Or you can start from the smaller number and count forwards to the bigger number. How many steps do you take? The answer is 5, because you go from 3 to 8 in 5 steps: **3, 4, 5, 6, 7, 8**.
She has 5 candies remaining. So we can write **8 - 3 = 5**.

Fill in the missing numbers:

1. 9 - 7 = ☐   **2.** 8 - 5 = ☐   **3.** 7 - 6 = ☐

4. 6 - 4 = ☐   **5.** 4 - 4 = ☐   **6.** 9 - 5 = ☐

7. 5 - 1 = ☐   **8.** 7 - 0 = ☐   **9.** 6 - 3 = ☐

10. Charlie accidentally drops and breaks one of his Mom's special mugs, and it has to be thrown away.
Mom had a set of 6 mugs. How many are now left?   _____

16

Once you have understood subtraction, award yourself a star in the box at right.

SUBTRACTING
TEST 6

In Class 2 there are 24 children registered. On Monday 3 children are absent. How many are present?

Yes, **21 are present**. Did you find the answer by counting backwards 3 steps from 24? Good. We can see the 3 steps like this: **24, 23, 22, 21**. You could also count forward from 3 to 24, but you would have to take 21 steps to do this!

The third way is to put the figures in the Tens column and the Units column, like this:

	T	U	
	2	4	In the Units column, 4 - 3 = 1.
−		3	In the Tens column, 2 - 0 = 2.
			So the answer is 2 Tens and 1 Unit,
	2	1	which is 21.

Try doing these in the same way:

1.	T	U		**2.**	T	U		**3.**	T	U		**4.**	T	U
	2	6			3	8			4	7			4	5
−		4		−		7		−		5		−	2	2

5.	T	U		**6.**	T	U		**7.**	T	U		**8.**	T	U
	5	9			3	6			7	2			8	4
−	1	8		−	2	5		−	5	1		−	4	2

9. Marina wants to buy a dress with a price tag of $69. The store manager tells her that she doesn't have to pay $69 because the dress is on sale and there is a reduction of $12. Marina is very happy to buy the dress. How much does she pay for it? _____

Putting figures into columns can be very helpful, but what do you do if the top figure in the units column is smaller than the figure under it? Let's look at this example:

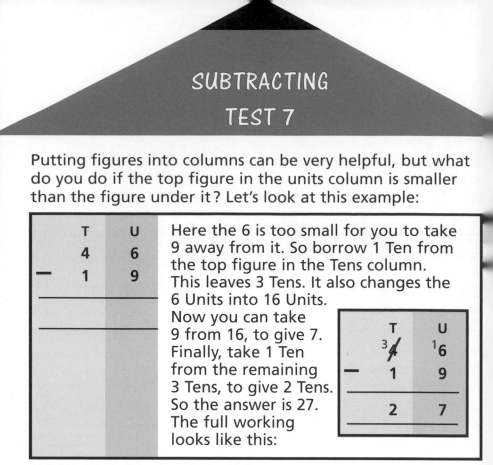

Here the 6 is too small for you to take 9 away from it. So borrow 1 Ten from the top figure in the Tens column. This leaves 3 Tens. It also changes the 6 Units into 16 Units. Now you can take 9 from 16, to give 7. Finally, take 1 Ten from the remaining 3 Tens, to give 2 Tens. So the answer is 27. The full working looks like this:

Follow this method carefully and you will score full marks on the test!

1.
T	U
5	5
− 2	8

2.
T	U
6	7
− 1	8

3.
T	U
2	2
−	9

4.
T	U
7	1
− 4	4

5.
T	U
8	4
− 5	5

6.
T	U
6	2
− 5	9

7.
T	U
9	1
− 7	6

8.
T	U
3	4
− 1	7

9. In a sale $15 is being taken off a calculator that normally costs $64. What is the sale price?

10. In a special offer you can save $28 on a train ticket that normally costs $73. What is the special offer price of this ticket?

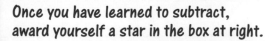

Once you have learned to subtract, award yourself a star in the box at right.

Suzie wants to buy 2 poinsettia plants. They cost $10 each. Suzie will need $20 to buy 2 plants. You can get this answer by adding $10 to $10. All you say is, "$10 + $10 = $20."

You can also get the right answer by multiplying. This time you say, "$10 times 2 is $20." Or say, "$10 x 2 = $20."

You can see that multiplying is a way of adding numbers that are all the same. When you have only two of them, like the poinsettia plants at $10 each, adding is as easy as multiplying.

But if Suzie wants to buy 8 plants it is rather slow and awkward to say, "$10 + $10 + $10 + $10 + $10 + $10 + $10 + $10 = $80." It is much easier to say,

$10 x 8 = $80

We can also set it out like this:

	T	U
	1	0
x		8
	8	0

To do these sums easily you need to know your times tables by heart – all the tables from 1 to 12.
If you know them already, you will find Test 8 easy.
You will also find them on pages 66 –76, so if you don't know them properly, this is a good time to practise!
Say them aloud to a member of your family, if possible.

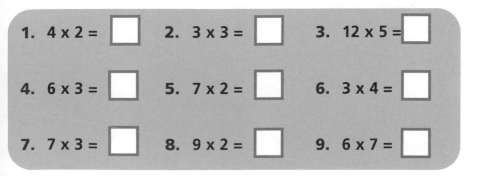

1. 4 x 2 = ☐
2. 3 x 3 = ☐
3. 12 x 5 = ☐

4. 6 x 3 = ☐
5. 7 x 2 = ☐
6. 3 x 4 = ☐

7. 7 x 3 = ☐
8. 9 x 2 = ☐
9. 6 x 7 = ☐

10. It costs $5 to go to the matinee movie. How much will it cost 4 friends altogether? _____

Once you have learned to multiply, award yourself a star in the box at left.

19

In our work on **ADDING** we met **carry-over figures.**
Do you remember? **When you get an answer above 9
in the Units column, you carry the first of the two figures
over to the Tens column and leave the second figure in
the Units column.**
We find the same idea of **carry-over figures** when we are
multiplying. Let's take, for example, **49 x 2**. First, put the
figures in the correct columns:

	T	U
	4	9
X		2
	9	8
	1	

Now multiply the 9 in the Units column
by 2, to get 18. Put the 8 in the Units
answer and carry the 1 to the Tens
column. Now muliply 4 x 2 to get 8 and
add the carried over 1 to give 9.
So the answer is 98.

All of the examples are like this. Sometimes the carry-over
figures are bigger than 1, but the method stays the same.

1.

	T	U
	1	4
X		3

2.

	T	U
	2	6
X		2

3.

	T	U
	1	8
X		3

4.

	T	U
	1	9
X		3

5.

	T	U
	1	9
X		4

6.

	T	U
	1	9
X		5

7. There are 24 pupils in Class 3.
To help pay for a field trip, each child
brings $3 to the class teacher. How much
is given to the teacher altogether? _____

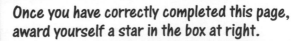

Once you have correctly completed this page,
award yourself a star in the box at right.

LONG MULTIPLICATION
TEST 10

Use long multiplication for numbers bigger than 12.
If you remember that there aren't any numbers bigger than 9, there's no problem. All you have to do is work methodically, as in all Math. Suppose you are faced with **327 x 245**.

This means: **327 x 5 units**
327 x 4 tens
327 x 2 hundreds

T/Th	Th.	H	T	U		
		3	2	7		
X		2	4	5		
	1	6	3	5	A	327 x 5 units
1	3	0	8	0	B	327 x 4 tens (write 0 in the units column)
6	5	4	0	0	C	327 x 2 hundreds (write 0 in the units and 0 in the tens column)
8	0	1	1	5		Add these 3 answers to get the grand total.

(Remember to carry the numbers over columns as you learned in the last exercise.)

1.

Th.	H	T	U
		8	3
X		2	6
	4	9	8
1	6	6	0
2	1	5	8

2.

Th.	H	T	U
		3	7
X		1	8

3.

Th.	H	T	U
		4	5
X		2	9

4.

Th.	H	T	U
	2	1	3
X	1	2	3

5.

Th.	H	T	U
	3	0	4
X	2	1	7

6.

T/Th.	Th.	H	T	U
		4	1	1
X		3	1	2

If you are an expert at multiplication, award yourself a star in the box at left.

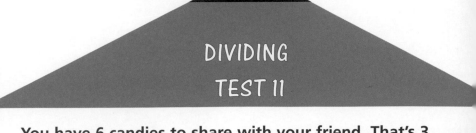

You have **6 candies to share with your friend. That's 3 each**, of course, because 6 divided by 2 is 3. You can write this as **6 ÷ 2 = 3**.

The teacher of Class 3 wants the **24 children to walk in pairs. How many pairs will there be**? Again, it is good to know the tables up to the 12 times table, because the question here is really **"How many twos in 24?"**
If you remember "12 twos are 24" then you know that **24 children make 12 pairs**. You can write this as **24 ÷ 2 = 12**. To check that you're right, you can multiply the answer (12) by the divisor (2) to get the first number (24): 12 x 2 = 24. You can see that multiplying and dividing are partners.

Here are some easy division questions. Simply fill in the answers:

1. $4 \div 2 = \boxed{}$	2. $4 \div 4 = \boxed{}$	3. $12 \div 4 = \boxed{}$
4. $20 \div 5 = \boxed{}$	5. $100 \div 10 = \boxed{}$	6. $54 \div 6 = \boxed{}$
7. $72 \div 9 = \boxed{}$	8. $60 \div 5 = \boxed{}$	9. $144 \div 12 = \boxed{}$

10. The 24 children in Class 3 are divided equally into 4 groups. How many children are there in each group? _____

11. In Class 3 the children sit 6 to a table. How many tables do they need? _____

12. The children of Class 3 are going to split into 3 equal groups for a quiz competition. How many will be in each group? _____

Once you have correctly completed this page, award yourself a star in the box at right.

This time you have **7 candies to share with your friend.**
As before, you can have **3 candies each,** but now **there is one candy left over. This candy is called the remainder.**
You can write this as **7 ÷ 2 = 3 remainder 1**
A simpler way of writing this is **7 ÷ 2 = 3 r1**

In this test all but one of the answers have remainders.
See if you can find the odd one out. Write the other answers as we did with **7 ÷ 2 = 3 r1**

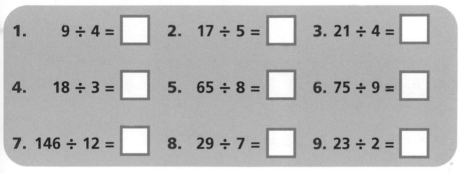

1. 9 ÷ 4 = ☐   2. 17 ÷ 5 = ☐   3. 21 ÷ 4 = ☐

4. 18 ÷ 3 = ☐   5. 65 ÷ 8 = ☐   6. 75 ÷ 9 = ☐

7. 146 ÷ 12 = ☐   8. 29 ÷ 7 = ☐   9. 23 ÷ 2 = ☐

10. Jane is planting 30 seeds. She is putting
4 seeds in each flower pot. How many
flower pots does she fill?   _____

11. How many seeds will Jane have
remaining?   _____

12. The restaurant manager seated his 60 guests
at tables. 8 guests could sit at each large
round table. The manager tactfully
arranged for a smaller table to be brought
for the guests who were "left over."
How many guests sat at the smaller table?   _____

23

TAKE A

GETTING THE MESSAGE

Hidden in the lines below are the letters you need to make up the Code Message. Clue: You are searching for numbers in the 4 times table. The letters that are with these numbers make up the words. There are 3 in the first line, to make up the first word, 4 in the second line and 5 in the last line.

22 18 15 (40) 3 59 12 81 82 36 74
A E F (N) H P O Z T W Á   (e.g. 4 x 10 = 40)

19 90 8 59 50 31 32 41 53 20 73 45 16
E H J O L V U I J S U X T

39 29 24 18 38 44 13 57 67 4 37 46 48 66 1 6 28 9
Q Z R T H E D G M L N P A C A R X J

Code Message:

N ☐ ☐   ☐ ☐ ☐ ☐   ☐ ☐ ☐ ☐ ☐

BREAK

GOOD HEALTH, MRS. JOHNSON!

Mrs. Johnson is interested in buying some good wine for a dinner party. The wine seller is telling her about a special offer in his store:

"Today you can buy any one of these cases – that's 12 bottles of absolutely beautiful wine – for $100. Or you can pay 5¢ for the first bottle, 10¢ for the second bottle, 20¢ for the third bottle, and so on, doubling the price for each bottle. So there you are. The choice is yours, Mrs. Johnson!"

Mrs. Johnson buys the wine and she saves money by making the right choice. Which method of payment does she choose?

_____

How much does she save?

_____

If you know your tables you can do a lot of dividing in your head. But if you have a big number to divide into, you can try **LONG DIVISION**.

Suppose you are asked to divide 684 by 4.
Here are the steps to follow:

STEP 1
Set the numbers down like this

$$4 \overline{| 6 \quad 8 \quad 4}$$

STEP 2
How many fours in 6? 1, remainder 2.
Write 1 above the 6, and 2 before the 8.

$$\overset{1}{4 | 6 \, {}^2 8 \quad 4}$$

STEP 3
How many fours in 28? 7, no remainder.
Write 7 above the 8.

$$\overset{1 \quad 7}{4 | 6 \, {}^2 8 \quad 4}$$

STEP 4
How many fours in 4? 1, no remainder.
Write 1 above the 4.

$$\overset{1 \quad 7 \quad 1}{4 | 6 \, {}^2 8 \quad 4}$$

So we can now write 684 ÷ 4 = 171

Try these long division questions in the same way, following all the steps carefully.

1. $5 \overline{| \, 7 \quad 5 \quad 5}$ 2. $3 \overline{| \, 4 \quad 8 \quad 9}$ 3. $4 \overline{| \, 7 \quad 2 \quad 8}$

4. $2 \overline{| \, 3 \quad 8 \quad 6}$ 5. $6 \overline{| \, 8 \quad 4 \quad 6}$ 6. $7 \overline{| \, 9 \quad 8 \quad 7}$

7. $8 \overline{| \, 9 \quad 6 \quad 2 \quad 4}$ 8. $3 \overline{| \, 7 \quad 5 \quad 3 \quad 9}$ 9. $5 \overline{| \, 6 \quad 8 \quad 2 \quad 5}$

10. The rancher had a herd of 5684 cattle. He sold a quarter of them. How many did he sell? _____
   Tip: A quarter is one of four equal parts of a whole.

Once you have got 100 per cent,
award yourself a star in the box at right.

You can also use this process of **LONG DIVISION** for dividing larger numbers.

Suppose you want to divide 23 into 483.
Here are the steps:

STEP 1
Set the numbers down like this

$$23\overline{)4\ 8\ 3}$$

STEP 2
How many time does 23 go into 4?
It doesn't. Move the 4 before the 8.

$$23\overline{)4\ ^48\ 3}\ ^0$$

STEP 3
How many 23s in 48? 2 r2.
Write 2 above the 8 and 2 before the 3.

$$23\overline{)4\ ^48\ ^23}\ ^2$$

STEP 4
How many times does 23 go into 23? 1 time exactly. Place 1 above 3.

$$23\overline{)4\ ^48\ ^23}\ ^{2\ 1}$$

So we can now write 483 ÷ 23 = 21

Try these long division questions in the same way, following all the steps carefully.

1. $15\overline{)3\ 4\ 5}$ 2. $13\overline{)2\ 9\ 9}$ 3. $14\overline{)3\ 0\ 8}$

4. $16\overline{)3\ 6\ 8}$ 5. $21\overline{)6\ 7\ 2}$ 6. $23\overline{)7\ 1\ 3}$

Once you have conquered long division, award yourself a star in the box at left.

Fractions, **decimals** and **percentages** are not as difficult as they may seem. They are all ways of describing parts of a unit.

A **fraction** means **a fragment or small piece**. It tells us how many parts of one unit, e.g. half a biscuit, two thirds of the class.

A **decimal** shows us how many **tenths, hundredths** and **thousandths of one unit.**
Two examples are:

Th	H	T	U		Tenths	Hundreths	Thousandths
			0	.	5		
	1	5	.	2	5		

In the first example you have **no units**, but **five tenths of one unit**. This is written as **0.5** (zero point five).

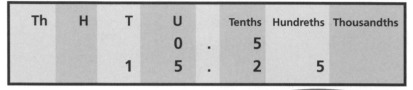

This is the same as a **half** or $\frac{1}{2}$ because **10 tenths equal one whole unit** and so **5 tenths is a half.**

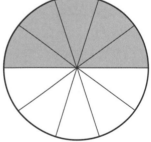

We can illustrate this in a pie chart. Here **ten pieces equal a whole unit**. We can describe the shaded part either as $\frac{5}{10}$ or **0.5** in the decimal form. Both answers show **a half of a whole**.

In the second example we have 1 ten, 5 units, 2 tenths and five hundreths. We read this as **15.25** (fifteen point two five). To illustrate this:

● ● ● ● ● We have **15 whole parts**
● ● ● ● ●
● ● ● ● ●

2 tenths (two parts of 1 whole).

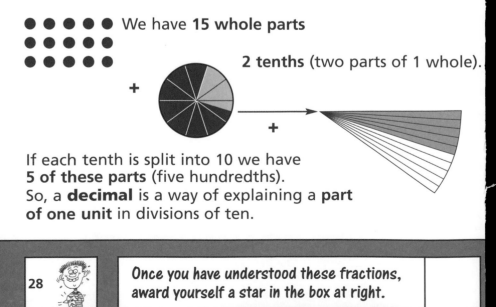

If each tenth is split into 10 we have **5 of these parts** (five hundredths).
So, a **decimal** is a way of explaining a **part of one unit** in divisions of ten.

Once you have understood these fractions, award yourself a star in the box at right.

A **percentage** tells us **how many out of 100**.
If you achieved **half marks** in an exam, we show this as **50%**
(50 out of 100 or fifty per cent).

$$\frac{1}{2} \quad 0.5 \quad 50\% \quad \text{are the same.}$$

To **change a fraction to a decimal**,
multiply the top number of the fraction by 10
and **divide the answer by the bottom number**.
Then **divide the answer by 10** by adding a 0 and a decimal
point at the beginning.

$$\frac{1}{2} \times 10 = \frac{10}{2} \longrightarrow 2\overline{)1\,{}^{1}0} = 5$$

Divide it by 10 by adding 0 and a decimal point at the
beginning = **0.5**

To **change a fraction to a percentage**,
multiply the top number of the fraction by 100 and **divide
the answer by the bottom number**. Remember to add the
percentage sign (%).

$$\frac{1}{2} \times 100 = \frac{100}{2} \longrightarrow 2\overline{)1\,{}^{1}0\ 0} = 50\%$$

To **change a decimal to a percentage**, simply **multiply the
decimal by 100** or **move the decimal point 2 places** to the
right to give the correct answer.

$$0.5 \times 100 = 50\%$$

**Show that you have understood by completing these
examples.** The first one is done for you.

Changing a fraction to a decimal and a percentage.

For example: $\frac{1}{2}$ 0.5 50%

1. $\frac{1}{5}$ ___ ___

2. $\frac{1}{10}$ ___ ___

3. $\frac{1}{4}$ ___ ___

If you have correctly completed the questions,
award yourself a star in the box at left.

29

ADDING & SUBTRACTING FRACTIONS
TEST 16

We know that a fraction has **2 numbers, one above the other**.

The top number is called the **numerator**, and the bottom number is called the **denominator**.

So in $\frac{1}{2}$ the **numerator** is **1** and the **denominator** is **2**.

When we want to add 2 fractions with the same denominator, we **simply add the 2 numerators** without changing the denominator. For example,

$$\frac{5}{11} + \frac{2}{11} = \frac{7}{11}$$

It's just the same with subtractions.

For example,

$$\frac{5}{11} - \frac{2}{11} = \frac{3}{11}$$

Try these in the same way:

1. $\frac{1}{15} + \frac{1}{15} = \square$

2. $\frac{2}{9} + \frac{5}{9} = \square$

3. $\frac{7}{11} + \frac{2}{11} = \square$

4. $\frac{4}{7} - \frac{1}{7} = \square$

5. $\frac{8}{17} - \frac{2}{17} = \square$

6. $\frac{4}{5} - \frac{1}{5} = \square$

7. $\frac{3}{17} + \frac{7}{17} = \square$

8. $\frac{11}{23} - \frac{9}{23} = \square$

Once you have completed this page, award yourself a star in the box at right.

But suppose you want to add $\frac{1}{2}$ to $\frac{1}{3}$. Now you have two different **denominators**. So these are the steps to take:

1. Find the lowest number that **2 and 3 both divide into exactly. This is 6**. This number is called the **Lowest Common Denominator** or **LCD**.

2. Take the first fraction ($\frac{1}{2}$). Divide the LCD (**6**) by the denominator (**2**) and multiply the answer by the numerator (**1**). This gives us 3 as the new numerator, and so we can express $\frac{1}{2}$ as $\frac{3}{6}$.

3. In the same way we can express the second fraction $\frac{1}{3}$ as $\frac{2}{6}$.

4. Add the new numerators **3 + 2** ($\frac{3}{6} + \frac{2}{6}$) to give the final answer: $\frac{5}{6}$

   The full expression is:

   $\frac{1}{2} + \frac{1}{3} = \frac{3}{6} + \frac{2}{6} = \frac{5}{6}$ If you want to subtract $\frac{1}{3}$ from $\frac{1}{2}$,

   use the same method:

   $\frac{1}{2} - \frac{1}{3} = \frac{3}{6} - \frac{2}{6} = \frac{1}{6}$.

Try these as well:

1. $\frac{1}{3} + \frac{1}{4} = \frac{}{12} + \frac{}{12} = \frac{}{12}$

2. $\frac{1}{4} + \frac{1}{5} = \frac{}{20} + \frac{}{20} = \frac{}{20}$

3. $\frac{1}{2} + \frac{1}{4} = \frac{}{} + \frac{}{} = \frac{}{}$

4. $\frac{3}{10} + \frac{2}{5} = \frac{}{} + \frac{}{} = \frac{}{}$

5. $\frac{1}{3} - \frac{1}{4} = \frac{}{12} - \frac{}{12} = \frac{}{12}$

6. $\frac{1}{4} - \frac{1}{5} = \frac{}{20} - \frac{}{20} = \frac{}{20}$

7. $\frac{4}{5} - \frac{1}{10} = \frac{}{} - \frac{}{} = \frac{}{}$

8. $\frac{1}{2} - \frac{1}{7} = \frac{}{} - \frac{}{} = \frac{}{}$

	Once you can add and subtract fractions, award yourself a star in the box at left.	31

When you want to multiply two fractions, **multiply the two numerators** (top numbers) and then **multiply the two denominators** (bottom numbers). It couldn't be easier.

Look at this example: $\frac{2}{3} \times \frac{1}{7} = \frac{2}{21}$

18 Multiply these fractions in this simple way:

1. $\frac{3}{5} \times \frac{4}{11} = \square$ 2. $\frac{4}{7} \times \frac{5}{9} = \square$ 3. $\frac{1}{3} \times \frac{2}{5} = \square$

4. $\frac{3}{7} \times \frac{1}{2} = \square$ 5. $\frac{1}{4} \times \frac{1}{5} = \square$ 6. $\frac{1}{2} \times \frac{1}{3} = \square$

7. $\frac{1}{10} \times \frac{3}{5} = \square$ 8. $\frac{1}{9} \times \frac{2}{3} = \square$ 9. $\frac{1}{6} \times \frac{1}{11} = \square$

When you want to divide one fraction by another, simply **tip the second fraction** (the divisor) **upside down, change the division sign to a multiplication sign**, and **go ahead as if you were multiplying**. If you can follow this example, you should have no trouble scoring full marks in this next test:

$$\frac{2}{5} \div \frac{1}{2} = \frac{2}{5} \times \frac{2}{1} = \frac{4}{5}$$

19 Work out the correct answers for these questions:

1. $\frac{1}{7} \div \frac{2}{9} = \frac{1}{7} \times \frac{9}{2} = \boxed{}$

2. $\frac{1}{9} \div \frac{1}{4} = \boxed{} = \boxed{}$

3. $\frac{1}{5} \div \frac{1}{2} = \boxed{} = \boxed{}$

4. $\frac{1}{3} \div \frac{2}{5} = \boxed{} = \boxed{}$

5. $\frac{2}{7} \div \frac{1}{2} = \boxed{} = \boxed{}$

6. $\frac{1}{8} \div \frac{2}{3} = \boxed{} = \boxed{}$

7. $\frac{3}{11} \div \frac{1}{3} = \boxed{} = \boxed{}$

8. $\frac{2}{7} \div \frac{3}{5} = \boxed{} = \boxed{}$

Once you have successfully completed the tests, award yourself a star in the box at right.

A circle is a beautiful shape.
It has a **CENTRE** and a **CIRCUMFERENCE**,
which is the boundary line of a circle.
Every point on the circumference
is the same distance from the centre
as all the other points.

A straight line from the centre to the
circumference is called a **RADIUS**.
The plural of radius is **RADII**.

A straight line going right across the
circle and through the centre is called
a **DIAMETER**. The diameter is twice
as long as the radius. The diameter
produces two angles of 180 degrees
each, which we write as **180°**.

If we take a quarter of a circle, we
produce a **RIGHT ANGLE**, like the
corner of a table. A right angle has
90°. The large angle that remains has
270°.

If we **BISECT** a right angle (cut it in
half), we have two angles of 45°
each. Each of these is an **ACUTE ANGLE**
(less than 90°).

The movement all the way around
the centre is **360°**. You can calculate
this by **adding the four right angles**
together: **90° + 90° + 90° + 90° = 360°**

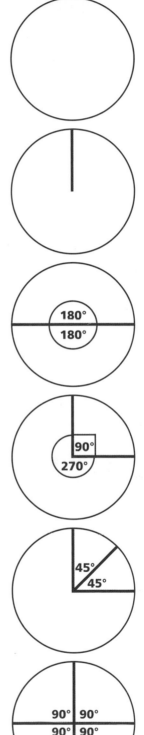

Once you have gone around in circles, award
yourself a star in the box at left.

33

The large hand of a clock (the minute hand) is like the radius of a circle. When this minute hand goes from 12 to 3, how many degrees does it pass through?

Yes, it passes through 90°.

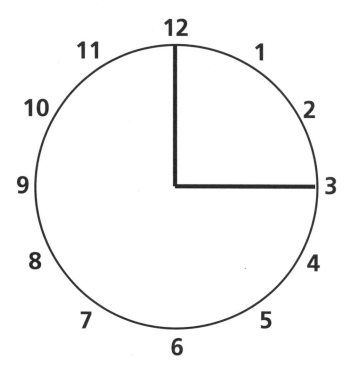

How many degrees does the minute hand pass through when it moves from:

1. 12 to 1 ? ( )   **5.** 12 to 7 ? ( )

2. 12 to 2 ? ( )   **6.** 12 to 9? ( )

3. 12 to 4 ? ( )   **7.** 12 to 11? ( )

4. 12 to 6 ? ( )   **8.** 12 to 12? ( )

We know that the diameter of a circle is twice as long as the radius. If the radius is 1cm, what is the diameter? **Yes, it must be 2cm.**

Once you have successfully completed these tests, award yourself a star in the box at right.

CIRCLES
TEST 21

Fill in the empty boxes.

	Radius	Diameter
Example	1 cm	2 cm
1.	**2cm**	_____
2.	**2.5cm**	_____
3.	_____	**6cm**
4.	_____	**7cm**
5.	**10cm**	_____
6.	**12cm**	_____
7.	_____	**100cm**
8.	_____	**1000cm**

Once you have successfully completed these tests, award yourself a star in the box at left.

35

A rectangle has four straight sides and four right angles.

This rectangle is 5cm long
and 2cm wide.

5 cm

90°   90°

2 cm

90°   90°

FINDING THE AREA OF A RECTANGLE
The area of a rectangle is all the space it occupies on the
paper. To find the area of a rectangle is very easy.

Multiply the length by the width: 5cm x 2cm = 10cm^2.

We read this as "**ten square centimetres.**"
You can see why the area of this rectangle is ten square
centimetres if you divide it into square centimetres,
like this:

5 cm

1	2	3	4	5
6	7	8	9	10

2 cm

Write the areas of these rectangles in cm^2.

	Length	Width	Area
Example	5 cm	2 cm	10 cm^2
1.	4cm	3cm	_____
2.	6 cm	1 cm	_____
3.	2.5 cm	2 cm	_____
4.	3 cm	1 cm	_____
5.	5 cm	3 cm	_____
6.	7 cm	6 cm	_____
7.	1.5 cm	1 cm	_____
8.	8 cm	7 cm	_____
9.	10 cm	3.5 cm	_____
10.	12 cm	11 cm	_____

Once you have understood your areas,
award yourself a star in the box at right.

On the previous page we looked at a rectangle 5cm long and 2cm wide. We calculated its area as 10cm^2. This means that half its area is 5cm^2.

Let's look at the rectangle again, but this time with a single **DIAGONAL** dividing the area into equal halves.

Each half is a **right-angled triangle**.

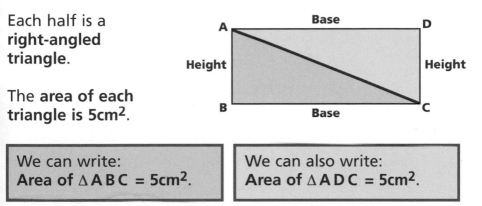

The **area of each triangle is 5cm^2**.

We can write:	We can also write:
Area of △ABC = 5cm^2.	Area of △ADC = 5cm^2.

We can understand why the area of a triangle is found by multiplying the base by the height and dividing the answer by 2.
So the formula for the area of a triangle is $\frac{1}{2}$BH (half the **BASE** times the **HEIGHT**).

Write the areas of these triangles in cm^2.

	Base	Height	Area
Example	5 cm	2 cm	5 cm^2
1.	4 cm	3 cm	_____
2.	6 cm	1 cm	_____
3.	3 cm	2 cm	_____
4.	7 cm	4 cm	_____
5.	2 cm	1 cm	_____
6.	8 cm	5 cm	_____
7.	5 cm	4 cm	_____
8.	6 cm	3 cm	_____
9.	10 cm	6 cm	_____
10.	8 cm	2 cm	_____

	Once you have understood triangles fully, award yourself a star in the box at left.	37

TRIANGLES
TEST 24

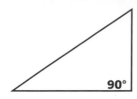

We have already met the **RIGHT-ANGLED** triangle.

An **EQUILATERAL** triangle has three equal sides and 3 equal angles.

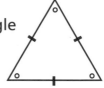

An **ISOSCELES** (say EYE-SOSS-A-LEES) triangle has two equal sides and two equal angles.

A **SCALENE** (SKAY-LEEN) triangle has no equal sides and no equal angles.

Now, an amazing fact about triangles is that the three angles always add up to 180°, no matter what shape the triangle is. So in an **equilateral triangle each angle is always 60°!**

If you know 2 angles, you can add them together and take the answer away from 180° to find the 3rd angle.

In this test we are told the first 2 angles of a triangle. What is the third angle?

	1st angle	2nd angle	3rd angle
Example	60°	20°	100°
1.	50°	50°	_____
2.	40°	40°	_____
3.	60°	40°	_____
4.	55°	75°	_____
5.	84°	63°	_____
6.	72°	91°	_____

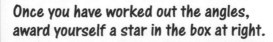

Once you have worked out the angles, award yourself a star in the box at right.

SQUARES
TEST 25

When a **number is multiplied by itself** the answer is called the **SQUARE** of that number.

> **So the square of 2 = 2 x 2 = 4 .**

It is called a **square number** because 4 dots can show the shape of a square –

The square of 3 = 3 x 3 = 9.
Nine dots can also show the shape of a square –

All the square numbers are like this.

A simple way to write the **square of 2** is 2^2.

The **square of 3** can be written as 3^2, and so on.

We read these numbers as **"two squared," "three squared,"** and so on.

Write the squares of the numbers.

		Square
Example	2^2	4
Example	3^2	9
1.	4^2	_____
2.	5^2	_____
3.	6^2	_____
4.	7^2	_____
5.	8^2	_____
6.	9^2	_____
7.	10^2	_____
8.	11^2	_____
9.	12^2	_____
10.	1^2	_____

If all your answers are correct, award yourself a star in the box at left.

39

A cube is the next step on from a square.

Multiply a square by the original number to find the CUBE of the number. For example,

> **the cube of 2 = 4 x 2 = 8**

What this shows is that the cube of 2 is really **2 x 2 x 2 = 8**.
It is called a **CUBE** because 8 dots can show the shape of a cube.

A simple way to write the **cube of 2** is 2^3, which we can read as "**two cubed.**"

The **cube of 3** is $3 \times 3 \times 3 = 27$.
The cube of 3 can be written as 3^3, which we can read as "**three cubed.**"

The cube numbers quickly become large, as we shall see in the Test.

Write the cubes of the numbers.

		Cube
Example	2^3	8
Example	3^3	27
1.	4^3	_____
2.	5^3	_____
3.	6^3	_____
4.	9^3	_____
5.	10^3	_____

Once you have worked out all the cubes, award yourself a star in the box at right.

Adding and subtracting are really important, so over the next few pages there are some more sums for you to work out.

Joe and James share a room. Joe has two pairs of running shoes and his brother James has three pairs. How many pairs are there in the closet every night if they always put them away?

If you know how to add up, all you need to do is say 2 plus 3 is 5. (You can also write this sum as 2 + 3 = 5.) So there are 5 pairs of running shoes in the closet each night.

Adding up is not difficult; and if you get lots of practice, you will soon know the answer to a simple sum like 25 + 38 without even thinking about it. (Yes, the answer is 63.)

See if you can do the test on the right. There are a lot of numbers; so if you do not make a mistake, you are doing really well. Even if it takes you a few attempts to get the correct answer, you are still making good progress.

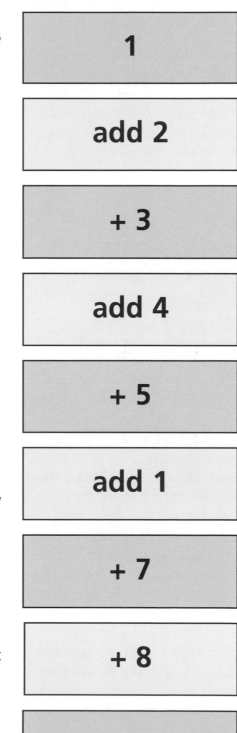

1

add 2

+ 3

add 4

+ 5

add 1

+ 7

+ 8

=

Once you have successfully completed this page, award yourself a star in the box at left.

41

MORE SETTING OUT

Remember, you will often find it easiest to write numbers you need to add up in columns, especially if any of the numbers have two or more figures. You can write out 26 + 13 + 14 = 53 in the following way:

$$\begin{array}{r} 26 \\ 13 \\ + 14 \\ \hline 53 \\ {}^{1} \end{array}$$

The answer goes under the line.

To do this sum, first you add the numbers in the units column on the right (6 + 3 + 4). If this came to 9 or less, you would write this part of the answer under the line in the units column. But it comes to *more* than 9: 13, in fact. So you write down the 3 under the line in the units column on the right and carry over the 1 (one ten) into the tens column to the left of the units column. Now you add up the figures in the tens column (the 1 you carried + 2 + 1 + 1). This comes to 5 and you write the 5 under the line in the tens column, to the left of the 3. So answer the is 53.

	H	T	U
			8
+			3
add			2
plus		2	3
+			9
+		3	7
+			5
add			2
=	?	?	?

Note: the column headed H is the hundreds column, T is the tens column and U is the units column.

42 Once you have correctly completed this test within 60 seconds, award yourself a star.

1

In Philip's piggy bank there are 5 quarters, 34 pennies, 28 dimes and 4 loonies. How many coins are in the piggy bank?

2

On the top shelf of Gordon's bookcase there are 21 books; on the shelf below there are 13 books; and on the bottom shelf, 29 books. How many books does Gordon have altogether?

3

On planet Zog, there are some strange animals. Dods have 3 legs each; Mops have 5 legs each; and Bots have 6 legs each. If there are two of each animal in a field, how many legs would there be in that field?

	H	T	U
			2
+		1	8
add			3
plus			7
+		2	5
+		1	0
+			1
add			4
+		1	5
=	?	?	?

Once you have successfully completed this page, award yourself a star in the box at left.

43

You already know that adding up is not hard with big numbers. You just follow the same way of working as with smaller numbers and prove yourself a genius! Look at 203 + 59 + 118, for example. Again, we can write down the numbers in a column.

$$263$$
$$59$$
$$+\,118$$
$$\overline{440}$$
$$\scriptstyle 1\ 2$$

In this sum, there is a units column (3 + 9 + 8), a tens column (6 + 5 + 1) and a hundreds column (2 + 1).

Starting with the units column, add 3 + 9 + 8. If this came to 9 or less, you could write it under the line in the units column. But it doesn't, does it? It comes to 20. So you write down the 0 under the line in the units column on the right and carry over the 2 to the tens column. Now add the tens column (2 + 6 + 5 + 1) and you will get the answer 14. So, as this is more than 9, put the 4 under the line in the tens column and carry the 1 to the hundreds column. Next you add the hundreds column (1 + 2 + 1) and get the answer 4.

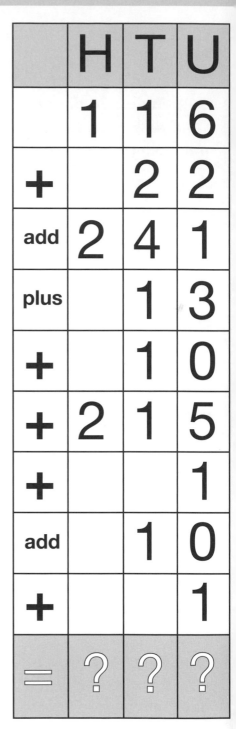

	H	T	U
		1	1	6
+			2	2
add	2	4	1
plus		1	3
+		1	0
+	2	1	5
+			1
add		1	0
+			1
=	?	?	?

44

Once you have correctly completed this test within 60 seconds, award yourself a star.

TEST 32	TEST 33
4	23
+ 218	plus 4
add 2	add 8
plus 5	+ 10
+ 311	plus 5
add 7	+ 564
plus 1	add 12
+ 28	+ 120
add 33	+ 13

Once you have successfully completed this
page, award yourself a star in the box.

Now let's try adding really big numbers that have a thousands column:
3473 + 2899. You can set out the sum like this:

$$3473$$
$$+\ \underline{2899}$$
$$6372$$

¹ ¹ ¹

First add 3 + 9 in the units column, which equals 12. As this is more than 9, write down the 2 under the line and carry the 1 to the tens column. Now add the tens column (1 + 7 + 9) and you get the answer 17. Write the 7 in the tens column and again carry 1, this time to the hundreds column. Now add the hundreds column (1 + 4 + 8) and you get 13. Write the 3 under the line and carry the 1 to the thousands column. Now add up the thousands column (1 + 3 + 2) and you get 6. Write this under the line in the thousands column. You now have the answer: 6372.
Once you can do this sort of sum without too much trouble, you are well on your way to becoming a mathematician!

1
In the number 506, which figure is in the hundreds column?

2
In the number 128, which figure is in the tens column?

3
In the figures 184 and 192, which figures are in the units column?

4
In the numbers 973, 318 and 26, which figures are in the tens column?

5
In the numbers 1380, 5907 and 632, which numbers are in the thousands column?

6
Which number is bigger: 6312 or 4513?

Once you have correctly answered these questions, award yourself a star in the box.

When you read English words, you always start from the left. When you add up columns of numbers, however, you always start at the right, with the units column. Then you take one step to the left to the tens column; one step further to the left, if necessary, to the hundreds column; and another step to the left, if necessary, to the thousands column.

When you are adding up big numbers, if the answer in one column is 0 or ends in 0 (20 or 60, perhaps), you need to be sure that you write down any 0 in an answer in the right place under the line. If you are not sure about this, look at this example:

```
  6337
+ 1765
  8102
  1 1 1
```

	H	T	U
	3	0	4
+		2	0
add		7	3
+		1	1
plus	1	4	9
+		3	8
+		4	5
add			9
=	?	?	?

Once you have successfully completed this page within 60 seconds, award yourself a star.

47

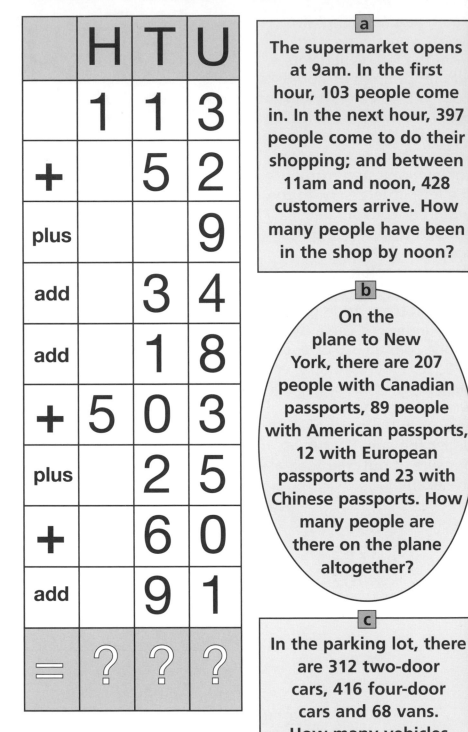

	H	T	U
	1	1	3
+		5	2
plus			9
add		3	4
add		1	8
+	5	0	3
plus		2	5
+		6	0
add		9	1
=	?	?	?

a

The supermarket opens at 9am. In the first hour, 103 people come in. In the next hour, 397 people come to do their shopping; and between 11am and noon, 428 customers arrive. How many people have been in the shop by noon?

b

On the plane to New York, there are 207 people with Canadian passports, 89 people with American passports, 12 with European passports and 23 with Chinese passports. How many people are there on the plane altogether?

c

In the parking lot, there are 312 two-door cars, 416 four-door cars and 68 vans. How many vehicles are there altogether in the parking lot?

Once you have successfully completed this page, award yourself a star in the box.

When you have an exam or a test at school, if you have time left over, it is always a good idea to check your answers. If you do this, you might be able to correct a mistake and get extra marks.

But if you think you have found a mistake, always double-check. Go through it once more, because you might have been right in the first place.

If you need to alter your answer, draw a line through it and put the correct answer by the side, above or underneath, wherever it will be clearest.

You need to write neatly because you cannot get marks for something that no one can read!

Never rush your work. It is easy to make a mistake when you hurry.

	H	T	U
	3	0	7
plus	1	5	1
+		3	8
add		9	2
+		2	0
+		1	6
+			4
plus		8	3
add	2	0	6
=	?	?	?

Once you have successfully completed this page, award yourself a star in the box.

49

Subtraction is just as important as addition, so here are some more sums!

John has 10 marbles and he gives James 4. How many marbles does John have left?

As you know, all you have to do with this sum is take away 4 marbles from 10 marbles. You can say 10 subtract 4, or 10 minus 4, or 10 - 4, or 10 take away 4. The answer is, of course, 6. (When you were smaller, you probably used to do this kind of sum using your fingers. If you want to do this sometimes, you still can. But with practice, you will find you can easily do this kind of sum in your head.)

We can also write out this sum like this:

$$\begin{array}{r} 10 \\ -\ 4 \\ \hline 6 \end{array}$$

Look carefully at the wording of the sums in TEST 39. Subtract 1 from 7, remember, means the same as 7 take away 1 or 7 - 1, or 7 minus 1.

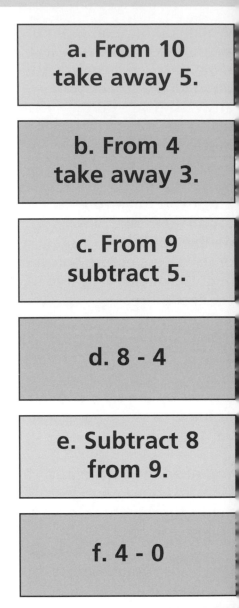

a. From 10 take away 5.

b. From 4 take away 3.

c. From 9 subtract 5.

d. 8 - 4

e. Subtract 8 from 9.

f. 4 - 0

g. Subtract 1 from 7.

h. 8 minus 3.

Once you have successfully completed this page within 60 seconds, award yourself a star.

Remember, if you have to do a subtraction sum with bigger numbers (perhaps 68 - 55, for example), you can set it out like this:

$$\begin{array}{r} 68 \\ - 55 \\ \hline 13 \end{array}$$

Just as you do when you are adding up, you have to start on the right in the units column. Say 8 take away 5, and you get 3. Write down the 3 under the line in the units column. Now move to the tens column. Yes, that's it: you go to the left. Say 6 take away 5, and you get 1. Write down the 1 under the line in the tens column. Now you have the answer written under the line: it is 13.

Try TEST 40 and see if you can get them all right!

a. From 15 take away 11.

b. 25 - 5

c. 42 - 31

d. 83 - 52

e. Subtract 27 from 38.

f. 48 - 22

g. Subtract 23 from 34.

h. 76 - 44

Once you have correctly answered these questions, award yourself a star in the box.

Sometimes when you are doing a subtraction sum, you will need to borrow from the tens column. Look at the following example.

$$
\begin{array}{r}
67 \\
-\ 39 \\
\hline
28
\end{array}
$$

As usual, you start with the units column. You cannot take 9 from 7, however, because 9 is bigger than 7. So you borrow from the tens column and turn the 7 into 17 by writing a little 1 at the side of it. At the same time, you turn the 6 in the tens column into a 5 because you have borrowed 1 from it to create the 17. Now say 17 take away 9 = 8, and write down 8 in the units column under the line. Next go to the tens column and say 5 - 3 = 2. Write the 2 under the line in the tens column. You now have the answer: it is 28.

a. 63 - 48

b. 52-39

c. Subtract 17 from 45.

d. 38 minus 29

e. Subtract 36 from 91.

f. 73 - 27

g. 93 - 48

Once you have successfully completed this page, award yourself a star in the box.

Look at this example:

$$\begin{array}{r} 124 \\ - 38 \\ \hline 86 \end{array}$$

Starting in the units column, you cannot take 8 from 4 because 8 is bigger than 4. So you borrow 1 ten from the tens column and turn the 4 into 14 by putting the borrowed 1 in front of it. At the same time, you turn the 2 in the tens column to 1 because you borrowed one ten from it. Now say 14 - 8 = 6, and write the 6 under the line in the units column.

Next look at the tens column. You cannot take 3 from 1 because 3 is bigger than 1. So now you have to borrow from the hundreds column. When you do this, you turn the new 1 in the tens column into 11. At the same time, you turn the 1 in the hundreds column to 0 because of what you have borrowed. Now say 11 - 3 = 8 and write down the 8 under the line in the tens column. In this sum, there will be nothing in the hundreds column because 0 take away nothing is nought. So the answer is 86.

a. 158 - 37

b. 504 - 28

c. 629 minus 84

d. From 527 subtract 39

e. Take away 147 from 312

f. 284 - 57

g. From 973 take away 129

Once you have successfully completed this page, award yourself a star in the box.

53

TEST 43	TEST 44
324	a. 46 + 74 + 11
+ 98	b. 329 - 179 - 83
- 32	c. 24 plus 98 + 32
plus 6	d. 67 + 813 + 701
- 12	e. 132 add 79 + 64
add 57	f. 108 minus 53
+ 29	g. 32 + 0 + 427
minus 103	h. 82 + 17 + 59
+ 43	i. 200 + 17 + 46

54 | Once you have correctly answered these questions, award yourself a star in the box.

a
In a movie theatre, there are 16 people in row A, 22 people in row B, 14 in row C, 18 in row D, 19 in row E and 21 in row F. The rest of the theatre is empty. How many people are in the theatre altogether?

b
Sixty-four of the people in the movie theatre buy popcorn. How many do not buy popcorn?

c
After the film, 20 people go home by car, 12 go by bus and the rest walk. How many walk?

d
Half of those who saw the film liked it. How many did not like the film?

160

plus 29

- 0

add 14

+ 136

minus 24

minus 83

plus 492

take away 39

Once you have correctly answered this page within 90 seconds, award yourself a star.

55

TAKE A

You have been working hard at all the tests so far, so it's time for some fun.

The dog in the picture is trying to find his way to the bone.
Can you find a path for him that adds up to 59?
Is it A, B or C?

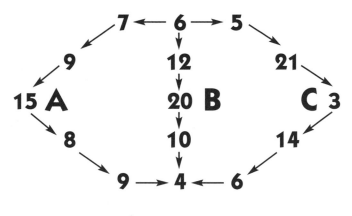

7 ← 6 → 5

9   12   21

15 **A**   20 **B**   **C** 3

8   10   14

9 → 4 ← 6

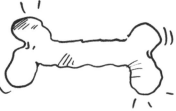

BREAK

All the practice you are getting in adding and subtracting should help with these.

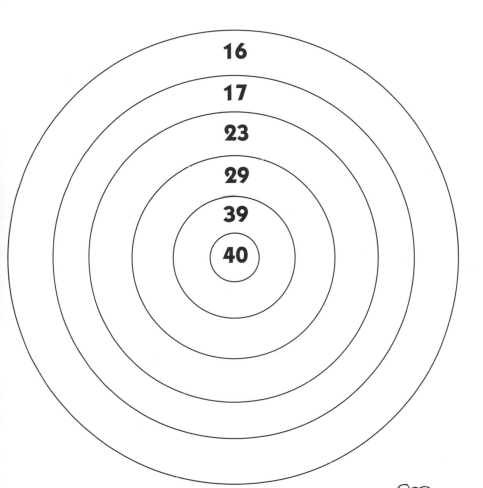

16

17

23

29

39

40

Paul was given an unusual darts game for Christmas. It comes with a series of challenges. One of these is to reach a score of 100 by throwing 5 darts. How can he do this? In another challenge, he has to get a score of 119 with only 3 darts. How can he do that?

1

A storekeeper wants to see how much he needs to order for his store.
He always likes to stock cans of soup but only has 54 on the shelf instead of 100. He likes to have 200 boxes of tea, but there are only 94.
There should also be 150 jars of jam but he only has 81.
How many
a. cans of soup
b. boxes of tea
c. jars of jam
should he order?

2

If a man walks 5 kilometres north, 3 kilometres east, 1 kilometre west and 2 kilometres south, how far will he walk in total if he goes back by the same route?

1001

+ 279

- 356

plus 4

minus 23

add 149

take away 12

+ 24

minus 32

58

Once you have successfully completed this page, award yourself a star in the box.

TEST 49

160

+ 32

- 98

+14

plus 83

minus 22

+ 64

add 31

+ 79

TEST 50

a

If there are 15 apartments on the ground floor, 18 on the second floor, 30 on the third floor and 20 on the fourth floor, how many apartments are there in the apartment building?

b

84 children leave a primary school at the end of the term and 73 new pupils join. There were 412 in the school to start with. How many will be there next term?

c

The party table has four kinds of sandwiches. On one plate, there are 18 ham sandwiches; on another, 10 egg sandwiches; on another, 12 cheese sandwiches; and on another, 14 tuna sandwiches. How many sandwiches are on the table altogether?

Once you have successfully completed this page, award yourself a star in the box.

59

TEST 51	TEST 52
a. 732 + 536	173
b. 804 + 799	add 68
c. 36 - 27	take away 22
d. 22 + 0 + 470	+ 339
e. 56 + 32 + 84	- 482
f. 63 - 29 - 15	plus 512
g. 181 - 97 - 36	+ 64
h. 110 - 11 - 47	minus 18
i. 68 + 3 + 12	+73

Once you have correctly answered these questions, award yourself a star in the box.

a

At the bank, they are counting up money. In one bag, there are 500 $1 coins. In another, there are 182, in another, 370, and in another, 148. How much money is there altogether?

b

Anne has $87 in the bank. On Monday, she puts in $22. On Tuesday, she takes out $41. On Wednesday, she puts in $53, and on Thursday, she takes out $15. How much does she have in the bank at the end of Thursday?

c

Mary is collecting books to sell for charity. Rod gives her 16 books, Penny gives her 19 books, Julie gives her 11 books and Robin gives her 18 books. How many books has Mary collected so far?

47
- 13
+ 183
add 19
- 22
+ 37
+ 252
- 10
plus 69

a

Jane spent 30 minutes doing her homework on Friday evening, 45 minutes on Saturday and 55 minutes on Sunday. How long did it take her altogether, in minutes?

b

Bobby said he would meet Jim at the station at 11:10am but he was 15 minutes late. What time did he get there?

c

A shoe store has 387 pairs in sizes 3, 4 and 5. 49 pairs are in size 3 and 112 pairs are in size 4. How many pairs are in size 5?

1

+ 111

+ 191

- 61

+101

take away 11

+ 13

minus 215

plus 131

Once you have correctly answered this page within 90 seconds, award yourself a star.

a. 63 + 24 + 108

b. 79 + 4 + 15

c. 419 + 23 + 18

d. 103 - 44 - 8

e. 37 + 93 + 24

f. 182 - 9 - 3

g. 704 - 192 - 8

h. 63 + 71 + 5

i. 82 + 0 + 54

a

John is looking forward to his holiday in 12 days' time. If today is March 14, on which date does he go on holiday?

b

If today is June 30 and Peter finished school 9 days ago, what date was the last day of term?

c

Polly lives at number 1 in her street. On her side, the numbers are all odd and run 1, 3, 5, 7, 9 and so on. On the other side, the numbers are all even and run 2, 4, 6, 8 and so on. Her best friend lives 10 houses away from Polly. What number does she live at?

83

- 72

+ 118

- 21

minus 38

plus 243

minus 29

+ 94

1
Rosie usually sleeps for 10 hours. If she goes to bed at 8pm, what time does she wake up ?

2
On Tuesday, Rosie went to bed at 8pm as usual, but woke at 1am and could not get back to sleep for an hour. If she slept for 11 hours that night, what time did she get up?

3
Robin is Rosie's little brother and he usually goes to bed at 7pm. If he sleeps for 12 hours, what time does he generally wake up?

4
If I borrow 8 books from the library on Monday, take back 3 on Tuesday, and take back 4 on Thursday, how many do I still have?

Once you have correctly answered this page within 90 seconds, award yourself a star.

a. 590 + 483	312
b. 672 + 711	-99
c. 98 - 49	add 47
d. 33 + 98 + 114	- 32
e. 63 + 84 + 92	+ 115
f. 111 - 52 - 38	- 74
g. 712 - 99 - 34	+ 83
h. 622 - 47 - 18	+ 570
i. 92 + 74 + 118	- 24

Once you have correctly answered these
questions, award yourself a star in the box.

a

There are 360 passengers on a ship. 49 get off at Athens, and another 27 at Haifa. How many passengers will then be left to continue the cruise?

b

Jack has a huge box of chocolates and the label says it contains 68 in all. On Saturday, he gives his mother 2, and eats 3 himself. On Sunday, he eats 2 and gives his friend 4. Later in the day, he gives his grandmother 4. How many does he now have left?

c

The book that Freddie is reading has 106 pages. He has read 81 so far. How many pages does he have left to read?

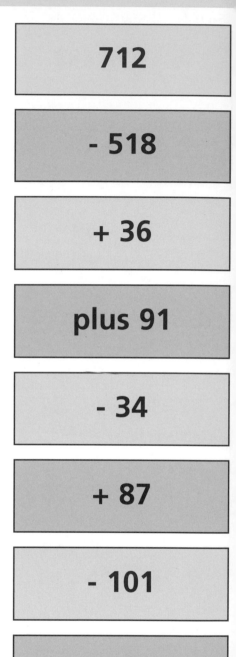

712

- 518

+ 36

plus 91

- 34

+ 87

- 101

+ 14

add 28

Once you have successfully completed this page, award yourself a star in the box.

a

If there are 1,480 people at a football game, and 365 are under 16, how many are 16 or over?

b

In the imaginary land of Skip, there are 5,740 men, 6,212 women and 3,110 children. What is the total population of the land of Skip?

c

Disaster! There were 540 eggs on the supermarket shelf but it collapsed and 318 broke. How many were left?

d

At the disco, Lucy danced 3 times with Harry, 4 times with Zak and 6 times with Colin. How many times did she dance altogether?

a. 61 + 99

b. 133 + 42 + 8

c. 173 + 99 + 24

d. 293 + 84 + 68

e. 27 + 183 + 98

f. 37 + 12 + 149

g. 136 - 10 - 27

h. 83 + 82 + 81

i. 67 - 12 - 18

Once you have successfully completed this page, award yourself a star in the box.

67

Now let's try something even easier. You already know 2 x 1 = 2. In fact, there is a rule that if you multiply any number by 1, it stays the same. Even 1,000 x 1 = 1,000. Here is your one times table. This is the easiest table to learn. Remember, no matter how big the number you multiply by one, it will always stay the same.

These sums will help you practise your one times table. There are also a few sums below to help you to review a table you should have already learned.

1 x 1 = 1
1 x 2 = 2
1 x 3 = 3
1 x 4 = 4
1 x 5 = 5
1 x 6 = 6
1 x 7 = 7
1 x 8 = 8
1 x 9 = 9
1 x 10 = 10
1 x 11 = 11
1 x 12 = 12

When you try the sums opposite, don't get caught out by 1 x 0. The answer is 0. In fact, any number x 0 = 0!

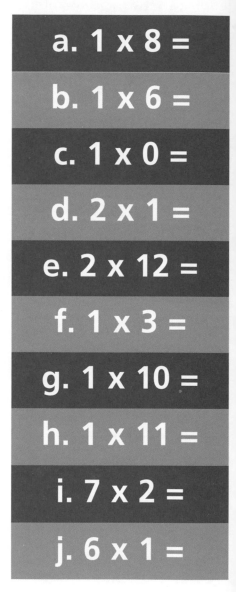

a. 1 x 8 =

b. 1 x 6 =

c. 1 x 0 =

d. 2 x 1 =

e. 2 x 12 =

f. 1 x 3 =

g. 1 x 10 =

h. 1 x 11 =

i. 7 x 2 =

j. 6 x 1 =

Once you have successfully completed this page, award yourself a star in the box.

Multiplication simply means a number added to itself several times.

Sometimes it is much quicker to multiply than to add up. What, for example, is the answer to the sum 2+2+2+2+2+2+2+2+2? It will probably take you a minute or so to get the right answer. If you count the 2s, you will find there are 9 sets of 2. If you know your 2 times table, you can say right away that 2 x 9 = 18.

Tables are blocks of numbers put together to make it easier for you to do multiplication and division sums.
Here is your 2 times table.

2 x 1 = 2
2 x 2 = 4
2 x 3 = 6
2 x 4 = 8
2 x 5 = 10
2 x 6 = 12
2 x 7 = 14
2 x 8 = 16
2 x 9 = 18
2 x 10 = 20
2 x 11 = 22
2 x 12 = 24

Look at the sums below, based on your 2 times table. See how quickly you can do them without looking at the table on the left.

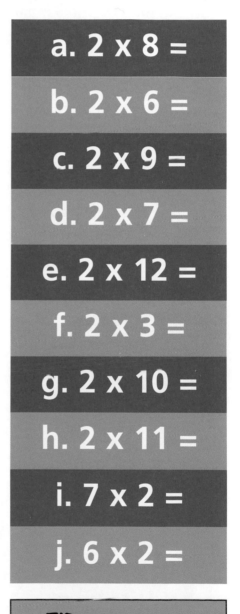

a. 2 x 8 =

b. 2 x 6 =

c. 2 x 9 =

d. 2 x 7 =

e. 2 x 12 =

f. 2 x 3 =

g. 2 x 10 =

h. 2 x 11 =

i. 7 x 2 =

j. 6 x 2 =

TIP: Times table is another name for multiplication table.

Once you have successfully answered these questions, award yourself a star in the box.

Tom has 3 cats, 3 mice and 3 hamsters. How many pets does he have?
Tom has 3 sets of 3. If you know your three times table, you will know at once that Tom has nine pets in all (3 x 3 = 9).

There were 7 people at Joy's party, including Joy. Each won 3 stickers. How many stickers were won altogether?
If you know your three times table, you will know at once that 21 stickers were won (3 x 7 = 21).

Now learn your three times table.

3 x 1 = 3
3 x 2 = 6
3 x 3 = 9
3 x 4 = 12
3 x 5 = 15
3 x 6 = 18
3 x 7 = 21
3 x 8 = 24
3 x 9 = 27
3 x 10 = 30
3 x 11 = 33
3 x 12 = 36

See how long it takes you to do these sums.

a. 3 x 4 =

b. 3 x 7 =

c. 2 x 7 =

d. 3 x 12 =

e. 9 x 3 =

f. 3 x 8 =

g. 3 x 0 =

h. 3 x 1 =

i. 11 x 3 =

j. 3 x 5 =

k. 2 x 3 =

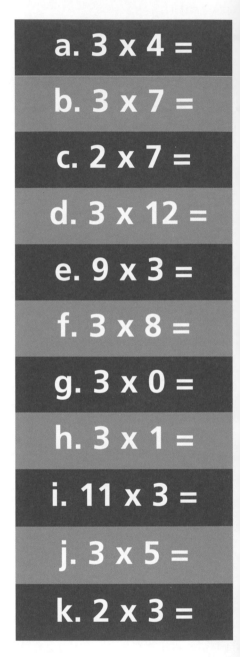

Once you have successfully learned your 3 times table, award yourself a star in the box.

Learning your 4 times table will also help you to do lots of sums, like these.

A team of 4 divers were searching a sunken ship for treasure. Each diver needed seven cylinders of oxygen. How many cylinders did they need altogether?
Answer: 28 (4 x 7 = 28)

A car runs for 11 kilometres on one litre of fuel. How far can it run on 4 litres?
Answer: 44 kilometres
(11 x 4 = 44)

Here is your four times table.

4 x 1 = 4
4 x 2 = 8
4 x 3 = 12
4 x 4 = 16
4 x 5 = 20
4 x 6 = 24
4 x 7 = 28
4 x 8 = 32
4 x 9 = 36
4 x 10 = 40
4 x 11 = 44
4 x 12 = 48

See how fast you can do all these sums this time!

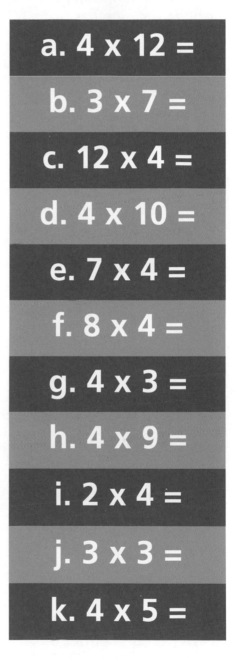

a. 4 x 12 =

b. 3 x 7 =

c. 12 x 4 =

d. 4 x 10 =

e. 7 x 4 =

f. 8 x 4 =

g. 4 x 3 =

h. 4 x 9 =

i. 2 x 4 =

j. 3 x 3 =

k. 4 x 5 =

Once you have successfully learned your 4 times table, award yourself a star in the box.

71

Lottie wants to buy five books at a book sale. Each book is 10¢. She has 50¢. Can she buy the books? 5 x 10 = 50, so Lottie *can* buy the books. If you know your 5 times table you will find it simple to do sums like this one.

Here is your 5 times table. Repeat it a few times and you will soon learn it.

5 x 1 = 5
5 x 2 = 10
5 x 3 = 15
5 x 4 = 20
5 x 5 = 25
5 x 6 = 30
5 x 7 = 35
5 x 8 = 40
5 x 9 = 45
5 x 10 = 50
5 x 11 = 55
5 x 12 = 60

Notice that whenever you multiply a number by 5, the answer ends in either 0 or 5. The even numbers (2, 4, 6, 8, 10, 12) end in 0 when multiplied by 5, and the odd numbers (1, 3, 5, 7, 9, 11) end in 5 when multiplied by 5.

Try the following sums.

a. 5 x 7 =

b. 8 x 5 =

c. 3 x 8 =

d. 5 x 6 =

e. 4 x 7 =

f. 4 x 5 =

g. 5 x 3 =

h. 2 x 7 =

i. 9 x 5 =

j. 5 x 12 =

k. 11 x 5 =

l. 8 x 5 =

Once you have successfully completed this page, award yourself a star in the box.

Now it's time to learn or review your 6 times table.

See how quickly you can do these sums. Try to do them in your head without looking back at your tables.

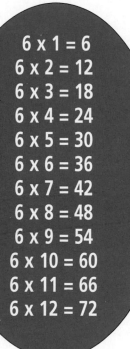

6 x 1 = 6
6 x 2 = 12
6 x 3 = 18
6 x 4 = 24
6 x 5 = 30
6 x 6 = 36
6 x 7 = 42
6 x 8 = 48
6 x 9 = 54
6 x 10 = 60
6 x 11 = 66
6 x 12 = 72

To test yourself on how well you know this table, it is a good idea to try to say it backwards, starting from 6 x 12 = 72. Try this with your two times, three times, four times, five times, ten times and eleven times tables as well. It will take a lot of concentration to get each table right!

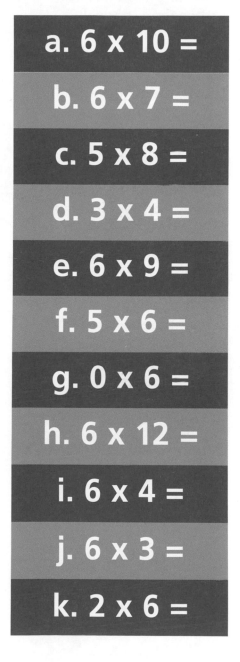

a. 6 x 10 =

b. 6 x 7 =

c. 5 x 8 =

d. 3 x 4 =

e. 6 x 9 =

f. 5 x 6 =

g. 0 x 6 =

h. 6 x 12 =

i. 6 x 4 =

j. 6 x 3 =

k. 2 x 6 =

Once you have correctly completed these sums, award yourself a star in the box.

73

There are 7 days in a week. If you learn the 7 times table, you can work out how far ahead in days rather than in weeks exciting things like your birthday or the end of term are. Then you can make charts, and check off all the days as they pass.

If something is in 6 weeks' time, for example, you just need to multiply 7 (the number of days in a week) by 6. $7 \times 6 = 42$, so there are 42 days in six weeks.

Here is your 7 times table. Practise it with a friend and see who gets it perfect first.

$7 \times 1 = 7$
$7 \times 2 = 14$
$7 \times 3 = 21$
$7 \times 4 = 28$
$7 \times 5 = 35$
$7 \times 6 = 42$
$7 \times 7 = 49$
$7 \times 8 = 56$
$7 \times 9 = 63$
$7 \times 10 = 70$
$7 \times 11 = 77$
$7 \times 12 = 84$

Ask someone to time you while you try these sums.

a. $7 \times 7 =$

b. $7 \times 2 =$

c. $7 \times 9 =$

d. $7 \times 4 =$

e. $6 \times 7 =$

f. $7 \times 8 =$

g. $7 \times 12 =$

h. $1 \times 7 =$

i. $5 \times 7 =$

j. $7 \times 3 =$

k. $8 \times 5 =$

Once you have successfully completed this page, award yourself a star in the box.

It you read aloud your 8 times table, given below, and repeat it a few times, you should soon be able to recite it perfectly.

The sums below include review of previous tables.

$8 \times 1 = 8$
$8 \times 2 = 16$
$8 \times 3 = 24$
$8 \times 4 = 32$
$8 \times 5 = 40$
$8 \times 6 = 48$
$8 \times 7 = 56$
$8 \times 8 = 64$
$8 \times 9 = 72$
$8 \times 10 = 80$
$8 \times 11 = 88$
$8 \times 12 = 96$

What's great is that each time you learn a new table, you will already know at least some of it. This is because you learned parts of it with the figures the other way around when you mastered earlier tables, for example, $8 \times 6 = 48$ and $6 \times 8 = 48$.

a. $8 \times 3 =$

b. $8 \times 6 =$

c. $3 \times 5 =$

d. $9 \times 8 =$

e. $4 \times 8 =$

f. $4 \times 9 =$

g. $8 \times 7 =$

h. $8 \times 10 =$

i. $8 \times 5 =$

j. $8 \times 8 =$

k. $8 \times 11 =$

l. $8 \times 12 =$

Once you have successfully learned your 8 times table, award yourself a star in the box.

75

If there are 9 skittles in a bowling lane, how many skittles would there be in a 12-lane alley?

9 x 12 = 108, so there are 108 skittles in a 12-lane alley.

Tony sleeps for nine hours each night. How many hours does he sleep in a week?

7 x 9 = 63, so he sleeps for 63 hours a week.

You can easily work out sums like these if you learn the 9 times table below.

9 x 1 = 9
9 x 2 = 18
9 x 3 = 27
9 x 4 = 36
9 x 5 = 45
9 x 6 = 54
9 x 7 = 63
9 x 8 = 72
9 x 9 = 81
9 x 10 = 90
9 x 11 = 99
9 x 12 = 108

Have a go at the following sums. If you have learned your 9 times table, they are a piece of cake!

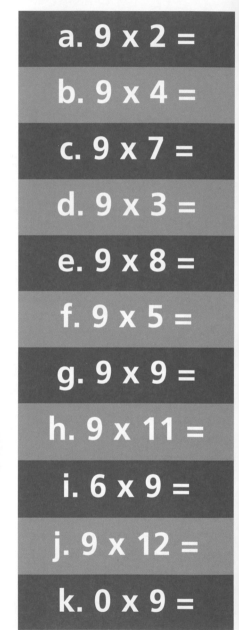

a. 9 x 2 =

b. 9 x 4 =

c. 9 x 7 =

d. 9 x 3 =

e. 9 x 8 =

f. 9 x 5 =

g. 9 x 9 =

h. 9 x 11 =

i. 6 x 9 =

j. 9 x 12 =

k. 0 x 9 =

TIP: All answers in the 9 times table add up to 9!

Once you have successfully completed this page, award yourself a star in the box.

Here is your 10 times table.

The following sums should not be difficult if you have learned your tables.

10 x 1 = 10
10 x 2 = 20
10 x 3 = 30
10 x 4 = 40
10 x 5 = 50
10 x 6 = 60
10 x 7 = 70
10 x 8 = 80
10 x 9 = 90
10 x 10 = 100
10 x 11 = 110
10 x 12 = 120

The 11 times table is also easy to learn.

11 x 1 = 11
11 x 2 = 22
11 x 3 = 33
11 x 4 = 44
11 x 5 = 55
11 x 6 = 66
11 x 7 = 77
11 x 8 = 88
11 x 9 = 99
11 x 10 = 110
11 x 11 = 121
11 x 12 = 132

a. 10 x 4 =

b. 8 x 10 =

c. 11 x 7 =

d. 5 x 11 =

e. 3 x 8 =

f. 2 x 9 =

g. 10 x 12 =

h. 10 x 11 =

i. 10 x 66 =

j. 1 x 10 =

k. 11 x 9 =

Once you have successful completed these sums, award yourself a star in the box.

A poultry farmer puts twelve eggs in a box. How many eggs will he need to fill twelve boxes?

12 x 12 = 144, so she needs 144 eggs to fill twelve boxes.

A café uses 12 litres of milk every day. It is closed on Sunday. How many pints does it use in a working week?

12 x 6 = 72, so the café uses 72 litres of milk in a working week.

Sums like this take only seconds if you know your 12 times table.

12 x 1 = 12
12 x 2 = 24
12 x 3 = 36
12 x 4 = 48
12 x 5 = 60
12 x 6 = 72
12 x 7 = 84
12 x 8 = 96
12 x 9 = 108
12 x 10 = 120
12 x 11 = 132
12 x 12 = 144

All of the sums below are based on your 11 or 12 times tables. See if you can get them all right.

a. 12 x 1 =

b. 12 x 10 =

c. 12 x 7 =

d. 11 x 8 =

e. 12 x 6 =

f. 12 x 4 =

g. 5 x 12 =

h. 4 x 11 =

i. 8 x 12 =

j. 12 x 9 =

k. 12 x 12 =

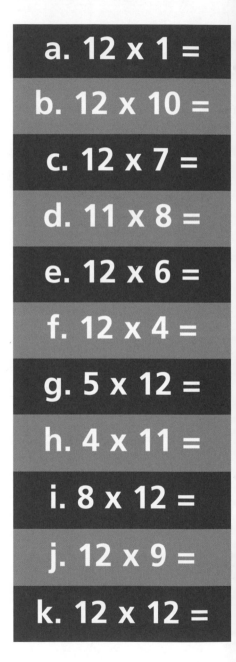

Once you have successfully learned your 12 times table, award yourself a star in the box.

Here's your chance to show off how well you have learned all 12 tables.

1 Amy is going to the zoo with Russell, James, Jade and Esther. Entry costs $3 each.
How much money will they need to get in?

2 Jim collects model cars.
He can fit 6 in each display case.
How many can he put in 9 cases?

3 Picture hooks come in packages of 5.
Dez bought 12 packs.
How many picture hooks did he get?

4 A bookcase needs 10 nails to attach each shelf.
There are 6 shelves.
How many nails will Dave need to build it?

5 Alexa earns $12 per week doing a paper route.
How much will she earn in 8 weeks?

Once you have correctly answered all the questions, award yourself a star in the box.

It's review time again! You should be able to do these sums quite quickly now.

a. 2 x 12 =

b. 3 x 6 =

c. 2 x 0 =

d. 4 x 7 =

e. 9 x 12 =

f. 2 x 3 =

g. 5 x 10 =

h. 2 x 11 =

i. 7 x 2 =

j. 6 x 8 =

k. 1 x 2 =

l. 9 x 3 =

Once you have correctly answered all the questions, award yourself a star in the box.

TEST 80

1 An ant has 6 legs.
Harry's ant farm has 8 insects that he can see.
How many legs can Harry see ?

2 Joanne's mother bought her 3 T-shirts at $12 each.
How much did she have to pay?

3 A pair of pigeons hatches 2 eggs at a time.
Mary has 6 pairs.
How many baby pigeons will she get?

4 David wants everyone to watch him play in a
big game. He is going on the team bus.
Six parents have cars, and each car holds 5 people.
How many people can come and cheer him on?

5 Tennis balls come in boxes of 6.
How many tennis balls are there in 6 boxes?

Once you have successfully completed this
page in 90 seconds, award yourself a star.

81

You must be getting very good at these tests by now. See if you can get all these right without looking back at any tables.

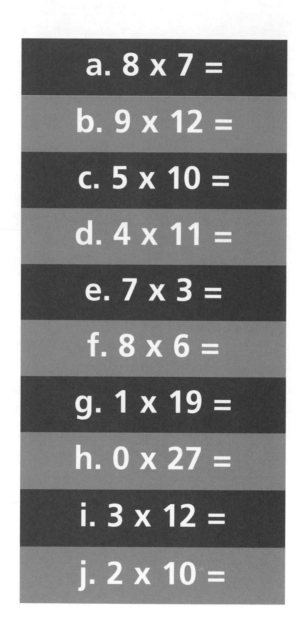

a. 8 x 7 =

b. 9 x 12 =

c. 5 x 10 =

d. 4 x 11 =

e. 7 x 3 =

f. 8 x 6 =

g. 1 x 19 =

h. 0 x 27 =

i. 3 x 12 =

j. 2 x 10 =

Once you have successfully completed this page in 90 seconds, award yourself a star.

1 The road builders outside Jemima's house have been there for 8 weeks. How many days is that?

2 If the road builders have to be there for another 2 weeks, how many extra days is that?

3 Ivan has 5 small boxes. He can fit 6 marbles into each box. How many marbles can he store this way?

4 Pencils come in boxes of 6. There are 36 children in Lisa's class. If the teacher buys 6 boxes, will she have enough for one pencil for each child?

5 Roses are put in bunches of 12. How many roses are there in 12 bunches?

Remember that multiplication sums are often set out like those below. Write out the sums in your notebook and give the answers under the line. Remember that x means multiply.

a. 8
x8

g. 4
x5

b. 9
x9

h. 3
x5

c. 4
x6

i. 2
x12

d. 5
x6

j. 11
x3

e. 3
x7

k. 12
x4

f. 6
x9

l. 12
x3

Once you have successfully completed this page, award yourself a star in the box.

83

TAKE A

**You have been working hard at all
the tests set so far, so it's time for some fun.**

Farmer Wilken keeps pigs and poultry.
Among his animals, the number of heads totals 64
and there are 170 legs in all. How many pigs and how
many chickens does he have?

BREAK

All the practice you are getting in multiplying and dividing should help with these.

1. Are you a genius? Can you do the following sum in under 30 seconds? Get someone to time you.

$$134 \times 843 \times 21 \times O \times 10 \times 46$$

2. If a man weighs 35 kilos x 2 ÷ 10 x 9, how much does he weigh?

Remember how if you have to multiply two numbers and either one or both are more than 12, you will need to use long multiplication? It is easy when you do it carefully step-by-step.

$$76$$
$$\underline{\times 6}$$
$$456$$
$$\scriptstyle 3$$

You do this sum by multiplying
6 by 6 = 36 (bring the 3 down)
7 x 6 = 42 + 3 carried from the last sum.
Answer is 456.

Apply these principles to long sums: 256 x 382
256 by 2
256 by 80
256 by 300
and then add the answers together.
Set out the sum like this:

$$256$$
$$\times \underline{382}$$
$$512$$
$$20480 \longleftarrow$$
$$+\underline{76800} \longleftarrow$$
$$97792$$

Put a 0 in the units column and multiply 256 x 80.
Put a 0 in the units and tens column and multiply 256 x 300.
So the answer is 97792.

Copy these sums carefully into your notebook, and do them there, setting out your working as shown below on the left.

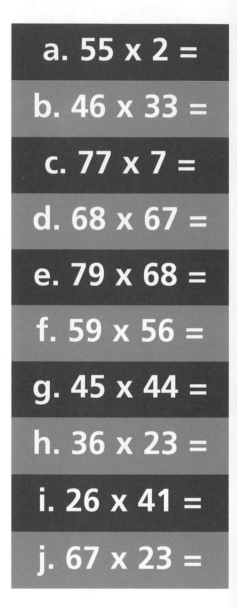

a. 55 x 2 =

b. 46 x 33 =

c. 77 x 7 =

d. 68 x 67 =

e. 79 x 68 =

f. 59 x 56 =

g. 45 x 44 =

h. 36 x 23 =

i. 26 x 41 =

j. 67 x 23 =

Once you have successfully completed this page, award yourself a star in the box.

LET'S DIVIDE!

We already know that division is simply multiplication the other way around. For example:

7 x 3 means that you have seven sets of three or three sets of seven. If you're not sure about that, lay out 3 lines of 7 counters, and then lay out 7 lines of 3 counters. You'll find that there are 21 counters in each of the sets.

You either have 21 counters *divided* into 3 sets of 7 or you have 21 counters *divided* into 7 sets of 3.

21 ÷ 3 = 7 and
21 ÷ 7 = 3

Look at the following examples, too.

4 x 5 = 20
So you know 20 ÷ 4 = 5
and 20 ÷ 5 = 4

6 x 3 = 18
So you know 18 ÷ 3 = 6
and 18 ÷ 6 = 3

8 x 4 = 32
So you know 32 ÷ 4 = 8
and 32 ÷ 8 = 4

7 x 9 = 63
So you know 63 ÷ 7 = 9
and 63 ÷ 9 = 7

Remember that division involves dividing one number into another number. Knowing how to divide will help you solve puzzles like this one.

A hotel decorator has 21 cushions to put in 7 rooms. How many cushions will each room get if they are divided equally?

To do this sum, you need to see how many times 7 (the number of rooms) goes into 21 (the number of cushions). 7 x 3 = 21, so each room will get 3 cushions. You have divided 21 by 7. The sign for division is ÷, so we can write this sum as 21 ÷ 7 = 3

TIP: When doing a division sum, you can always check if you have got the answer right by multiplying the answer by the number you are dividing by. You should end up with the number at the beginning of the sum. For example:

63 ÷ 9 = 7
Check: 7 x 9 = 63

Once you have fully understood this page, award yourself a star in the box.

87

Knowing how to divide can be very useful if you need to share things out. Take a look at the following examples.

Jim has $40. How many computer games can he buy at $10 each?

40 ÷ 10 = 4, so Jim can buy 4 games.

Marilyn has 36 baby gerbils. How many friends can have 4 each?

36 ÷ 4 = 9, so Marilyn can give 9 friends 4 gerbils each.

Dad made 26 sandwiches for Jim, Joe and Jon. What was the most even way of sharing them between the three boys?

26 ÷ 3 = 8 remainder 2, so each boy got 8 sandwiches, and Dad ate the two that were left over!

Alison has 13 books that she wants to give to 3 different charity shops. How can she divide them up most fairly?

13 ÷ 3 = 4 with 1 over. So two charity shops get 4 books and one gets 5 books.

1 A sports foundation got a gift of $380. A football costs $19. How many could the club buy?

2 Twenty people won a competition where the prize was $400. How much was each winner's share?

3 A man wanted to share $144 equally between his 12 grandchildren. How much did he give each one?

4 There are 165 crates of tea landing in Littlebay every day. If there are 11 ships, how many crates does each ship carry?

Use the multiplication grid on page 98 to help you with these sums.

Once you have successfully completed this page, award yourself a star in the box.

Lay out 2 rows of 3 counters. If you add 1 counter to one row, you will now have 7 counters in all.

But no matter how you arrange 7 counters, you cannot make rows of the same length. This is because 7 does not divide exactly. As we've already seen, it has a *remainder*. There is something left over.

There is always a bit left over in the following sums too. It is called the *remainder* but you can call it 'r' to save time, if you like.

$17 \div 5 = 3$ remainder 2
$29 \div 3 = 9$ r 2
$48 \div 9 = 5$ r 3
$22 \div 7 = 3$ r 1

TIP: If the remainder is bigger than the number you are dividing by, try again! Something has gone wrong.

Copy these sums carefully into your book. You will find that they all have remainders. Give the remainder in your answers.

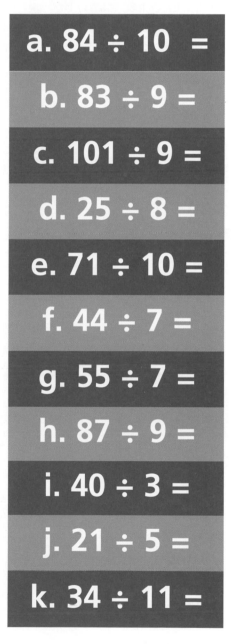

a. $84 \div 10 =$

b. $83 \div 9 =$

c. $101 \div 9 =$

d. $25 \div 8 =$

e. $71 \div 10 =$

f. $44 \div 7 =$

g. $55 \div 7 =$

h. $87 \div 9 =$

i. $40 \div 3 =$

j. $21 \div 5 =$

k. $34 \div 11 =$

Once you have correctly answered these questions in 60 seconds, award yourself a star.

89

6)42 means that the number under the line, 42, is being divided by the number on the left, 6.

So 24 ÷ 12 = 2 can also be written

$$\begin{array}{r} 2 \\ 12\overline{)24} \end{array}$$

The answer is written above the line. Here are a few more examples.

48 ÷ 12 = 4 can also be written as

$$\begin{array}{r} 4 \\ 12\overline{)48} \end{array}$$

54 ÷ 9 = 6 can also be written as

$$\begin{array}{r} 6 \\ 9\overline{)54} \end{array}$$

Copy the sums given below into your notebook, setting them out as in the method given opposite. Don't rush until you are sure of what you are doing. You will find the 13–20 times table grid

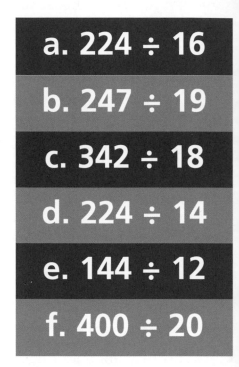

a. 224 ÷ 16

b. 247 ÷ 19

c. 342 ÷ 18

d. 224 ÷ 14

e. 144 ÷ 12

f. 400 ÷ 20

on page 98 very helpful.

Remember, the number you are dividing is known as the *dividend*. The number you are dividing *by* is the *divisor*; and the answer is the *quotient*. So in 27÷3 = 9, 27 is the *dividend*, 3 is the *divisor*, and 9 is the *quotient*.

Once you have successfully completed this page, award yourself a star in the box.

We already know that long division is used for dividing large numbers. Here is another example. We set the sum out as before.

$$\frac{24}{16)384}$$

To do this sum, start from the left. You have to think of 384 in single figures. First try 16 into 3. It will not divide, because 16 is more than 3, so try using the 8 as well. See how 16 divides into 38. 16 x 2 = 32, so you write the 2 on the top line. Now take 32 away from 38. (38 − 32 = 6). Sixteen into 6 will not divide, again because 16 is bigger than 6. So bring down the 4 from the top line, and put it next to the 6 to make 64. 64 ÷ 16 = 4. Write the 4 on the top line and take the 64 away. There is no remainder, so the answer is 24. The working is set out below. Follow it through.

$$\frac{24}{16)384}$$
$$\underline{32}$$
$$64$$
$$\underline{64}$$
$$00$$

Copy these sums into your notebook. You will pick up speed as you continue to do these sums. Remember, in the middle or at the end of your division sum, if a number cannot be divided, put a 0 on the line to say so.

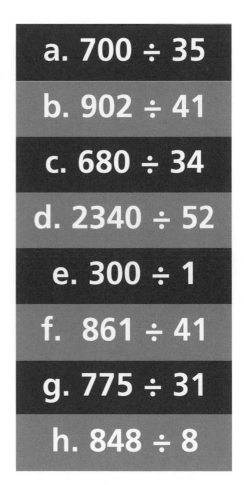

a. 700 ÷ 35

b. 902 ÷ 41

c. 680 ÷ 34

d. 2340 ÷ 52

e. 300 ÷ 1

f. 861 ÷ 41

g. 775 ÷ 31

h. 848 ÷ 8

Once you have successfully completed this page, award yourself a star in the box.

91

1 Bea has 200 CDs. At the moment, they are all over her bedroom floor. How many racks does she need if each holds 25 CDs?

2 A pizzeria buys jars of pizza sauce in boxes of 32. They need 1440 jars per month. How many boxes is that?

3 Yummyspud sells 420 baked potatoes each day. How many days does it take them to sell 2,940 potatoes?

4 An Australian sheep farmer put his 2,295 sheep into pens for their annual shearing. He put 85 sheep into each pen. How many pens did he have?

5 17 workers in a garment factory sewed on 5,780 buttons a day. How many did each worker sew on?

  Once you have successfully completed this page, award yourself a star in the box.

You will have to think a bit more while you do these sums, but they are not really much harder. Copy them into your notebook, leaving plenty of space underneath them to write all your working out. Remember to show any remainder.

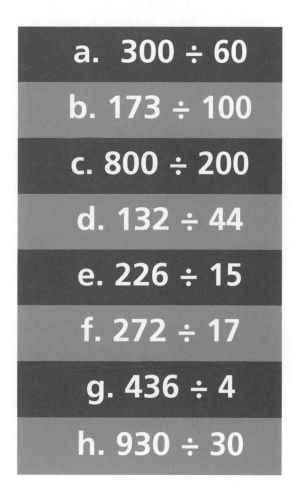

a. 300 ÷ 60

b. 173 ÷ 100

c. 800 ÷ 200

d. 132 ÷ 44

e. 226 ÷ 15

f. 272 ÷ 17

g. 436 ÷ 4

h. 930 ÷ 30

Once you have successfully completed this page, award yourself a star in the box, left.

93

TEST 91

1 Serge goes to and from school by bus.
Each way is 6 kilometres. He never goes to school
on weekends. How many kilometres does he travel
on the bus each week? Remember, he goes to school
and back home.

2 An octopus has 8 arms with suction pads on the
underside. If each arm can stick to 3 fish, how many
fish can the octopus hold onto at once?

3 There are three movie theatres in the town
where Janey lives. Each theatre shows 8 films
per week. How many films get shown?

4 Sam loves apples.
He eats 4 a day. How many apples does
he eat in a week?

Once you have successfully completed this
page, award yourself a star in the box.

Copy these sums into your book. You should be able to do them quite quickly, but you must still think hard about what you are doing if you are going to get all of them right.

a. 34 x 4	b. 56 x 9
c. 81 x 7	d. 111 x 1
e. 235 x 4	f. 879 x 6
g. 361 x 5	h. 553 x 3
i. 943 x 7	j. 621 x 32
k. 31 x 0	l. 68 x 20

Once you have successfully completed this page, award yourself a star in the box, left.

95

Here are some more puzzles. Can you solve them all?

1 A supermarket chain is giving out tokens for school supplies. 90 tokens are needed for one book. How many books can a school get for 2,880 tokens?

2 There are 38 nails in a package. If Tony needs 646 nails, how many packages should he buy?

3 If a family of 4, eating three meals a day, eats 12 meals a day between them, how many meals will the family eat in a leap year? A leap year has 366 days.

4 An adult has 32 teeth. How many teeth should a football team's 11 players have between them?

Once you have successfully completed this page, award yourself a star in the box.

If you know all your tables and have worked right through this book, you should find that the following sums are not difficult at all.

a. 1,842 x 5 x 0

b. 9,999,999 x 1

c. 1,000 ÷ 100

d. 300 ÷ 50

e. 144 ÷ 12

f. 49 ÷ 7

g. 289 ÷ 17

h. 1,000 ÷ 25

i. 1,000 ÷ 20

j. 2940 ÷ 7

Once you have successfully completed this page, award yourself a star in the box, left.

97

MULTIPLICATION GRID

You will find the grid below useful for when you need to multiply numbers from 13 to 20. Find one of the numbers you are multiplying in the left-hand column and the other in the top row. Then follow each along until they meet. The number in that square is the answer.

	13	14	15	16	17	18	19	20
1	13	14	15	16	17	18	19	20
2	26	28	30	32	34	36	38	40
3	39	42	45	48	51	54	57	60
4	52	56	60	64	68	72	76	80
5	65	70	75	80	85	90	95	100
6	78	84	90	96	102	108	114	120
7	91	98	105	112	119	126	133	140
8	104	112	120	128	136	144	152	160
9	117	126	135	144	153	162	171	180
10	130	140	150	160	170	180	190	200
11	143	154	165	176	187	198	209	220
12	156	168	180	192	204	216	228	240
13	169	182	195	208	221	234	247	260
14	182	196	210	224	238	252	266	280
15	195	210	225	240	255	270	285	300
16	208	224	240	256	272	288	304	320
17	221	238	255	272	289	306	323	340
18	234	252	270	288	306	324	342	360
19	247	266	285	304	323	342	361	380
20	260	280	300	320	340	360	380	400

There are millions and millions of different kinds of **living things** in the world. **Some are very big like trees, whales and elephants** and **some are very small like ants, bacteria and viruses.** Not everything in the world is alive. For example, stones, water and cars are not alive.

Non-living   *Living*   *Living*

The main difference between living things and non-living things is that living things can:

> breathe   grow and reproduce   move about
> sense things around them
> they all need food to survive

1. From the list below write down the things that:

   a. animals can do   **b.** a car can do   **c.** a plant can do

_____   _____   _____

_____   _____   _____

_____   _____   _____

_____   _____   _____

> move from place to place   breathe
> reproduce   make their own food
> heal themselves when they get damaged
> grow   eat food

2. Put the following things into two groups: **living** and **non-living**:

   elephant,   microwave oven,   stream,   bicycle,
     oak tree,   human being,   bottle,   train,
         bee,   cat,   fish,   glass

Living   **Non-living**

_____   _____

_____   _____

_____   _____

_____   _____

_____   _____

Now that you know all about living and non-living things, award yourself a star in the box.

THE FOOD CHAIN
TEST 2

All living things need food for energy and growth.
Plants make their own food but animals can't. This means that animals have to get their food from elsewhere. Plants serve as food for most animals, even if they don't eat them directly. For example, a worm eats leaves and other bits of plants; the worm is eaten by a bird and the bird is eaten by a cat. Although the cat and the bird don't eat the plant themselves, they still depend on it to survive.
   This is called a food chain. The food chain shows how food is passed from the leaf to the worm and then on to the bird.

Animals that eat plants are called herbivores.
Animals that eat other animals are called carnivores.
Animals that eat plants and animals are called omnivores.

1. Foxes eat rabbits; carrots are plants that make their own food; rabbits eat carrots.
a. Draw a food chain to show this information.

b. Which animal in this food chain is a herbivore?
_____

c. What would happen to the foxes if the rabbits died?
_____

2. What is the difference between an omnivore and a carnivore?
_____

3. Look at this list of living things. For each one say whether it is a plant, a herbivore or a carnivore:

   a. grass   b. sheep   c. dog
   _____   _____   _____

   d. lion   e. deer   f. rosebush
   _____   _____   _____

Once you have understood how a food chain works, award yourself a star in the box.

101

ANIMALS AND FOOD
TEST 3

Humans are animals. There are millions of different types of animal in the world but they all have certain features in common. For example, **all animals have to eat food because they can't make food in their own bodies,** like plants can.

Humans (including you) are animals, and like all animals you need to eat food every day to stay alive. Food has three important functions in your body:

to give you energy	to help you grow	to keep you healthy

1. Why do all animals have to eat food?
   _____

2. Why don't plants have to eat food?
   _____

3. Almost all food is good for you, but some can be harmful if you eat too much. Look at this list of food and drink:

Cola drink	Milk	Bread	Baked beans
Fruit	Potatoes	Chocolate	French fries
Eggs	Potato chips	Hamburger	Vegetables

a. Which of these is it good to have lots of every day?
   _____

b. Which should you have only very occasionally?
   _____

c. Which are very good for you, but you don't need them every day?
   _____

102

Now that you know what you should and shouldn't eat, award yourself a star in the box.

ANIMAL ADAPTATIONS
TEST 4

Another feature common to animals is that they can all move around from place to place. However, they all have very different features depending on how and where they live – this is called adaptation. For example:

Fish are adapted to live in the sea.
They have a tail and fins that allow them to swim and gills that allow them to get oxygen from the water so they can breathe.

Cats are adapted to live on land.
They have legs that allow them to walk and run; claws to help them climb trees and catch prey; and lungs to breathe air.

---

1. Link these features with the animal's activity:

1 fur		**a** walking and running
2 claws		**b** climbing trees
3 teeth		**c** flying
4 legs		**d** breathing air
5 gills		**e** breathing under water
6 wings		**f** swimming
7 lungs		**g** keeping warm
8 fins		**h** eating food

2. Wolves live in cold places and they eat mice and caribou. Choose five adaptations from the list above that wolves have.

_____

3. Butterflies and birds all have wings.
What does this tell you about how they move around ? _____

4. Whales live in the sea but they have lungs, not gills.
What does this tell you about how they breathe ?

_____

5. Bats have fur, wings, lungs and teeth. What does this tell you about how they live ?

_____

When you can identify an animal's lifestyle by its adaptations, award yourself a star in the box.

103

HEART AND BLOOD
TEST 5

Blood is a very important fluid that carries food and oxygen around your body. This food and oxygen is vital to your organs, brain and muscles. The blood is kept moving by a special pump called your **heart**, which is found in the middle of your chest and slightly to the left. Your heart is made of muscle and is about the size of your clenched fist.

When the heart muscle contracts (gets smaller) it pushes blood out of the heart and the blood travels to all parts of your body in tubes called arteries. When the heart muscle relaxes, blood flows back into it through tubes called veins.

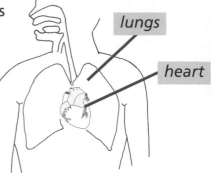

lungs

heart

Like other muscles and organs in your body, your heart needs to be looked after and there are a few things to remember:

Do not smoke | **Eat a balanced diet** | **Take regular exercise**

1. What happens when your heart contracts?
   _____

2. Match these words with their functions:
   1 heart   **a** carries blood back to the heart
   2 blood   **b** pumps blood around the body
   3 artery   **c** carries food and oxygen around the body
   4 vein   **d** carries blood away from the heart

3. How does food and oxygen travel around your body?
   _____

4. Which of the following are **good** for your heart and **bad** for your heart
   a. drinking lots of beer __ **b.** walking to the store __
   c. eating fruit and vegetables ___ **d.** smoking ___
   e. eating doughnuts ___ **f.** driving to the mall ___
   g. 10 minutes of skipping every day ___

Once you know all about the heart, award yourself a star in the box.

PULSE AND HEARTBEAT
TEST 6

Every time your heart contracts, it is known as a **heartbeat**. You can feel this movement by putting your hand on your heart or by feeling the pulse on your neck or your wrist. By counting your pulse you can measure how many heartbeats you have each minute.

Your heart beats at different rates depending on what you are doing. Exercise makes your heart beat faster. This is because your muscles work very hard during exercise and they need lots of food and oxygen to keep them working. So your heart beats faster, pumping blood around the body to deliver this food to where it is needed. When you stop exercising, your muscles begin to recover and don't need as much food and oxygen, so your heart slows down. Eventually it drops to its normal heartbeat rate, called the **resting rate**.

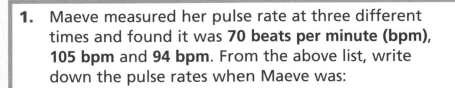

---

1. Maeve measured her pulse rate at three different times and found it was **70 beats per minute (bpm)**, **105 bpm** and **94 bpm**. From the above list, write down the pulse rates when Maeve was:

   a. exercising _____

   b. resting _____

   c. sitting down just after exercising _____

2. What happens to your pulse rate when you exercise?
   _____

3. Which part of your body needs extra food and oxygen when you exercise?
   _____

4. Maeve's pulse got faster when she exercised for five minutes. What is his pulse the measure of?
   _____

If you can take your pulse and understand what it means, award yourself a star in the box.

105

BREATHING
TEST 7

The air around us is made up of lots of different gases.
**One particular gas is very important as we use it in our
bodies to help us get energy from our food.
This gas is called oxygen.**

When we breathe in, air is taken into
our lungs and some of the oxygen
in the air is absorbed into the blood
that carries the oxygen around
the body.

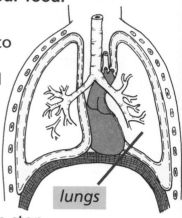

lungs

When we are relaxed we breathe
at a rate of about 12 to 14 breaths
per minute. But if we start to
exercise, our breathing rate speeds
up, then slows down again when we stop.

1. Whereabouts in your body are your lungs found?

   a. chest   **b.** head   **c.** abdomen

2. What do we use oxygen for in our bodies?

   _____

3. How is oxygen carried to all parts of the body?

   _____

4. This graph shows
   Stella's breathing rate
   when she is resting,
   then when she starts
   to exercise and when
   she stops exercising.

   Breathing rate (bpm) — 40, 30, 20, 10

   Time (min) — 2 4 6 8 10 12

   a. Between 0-2 minutes, was
   Stella resting or exercising? _____

   b. At what time did Stella start to exercise? _____

   c. What happened to her breathing rate
   when she was exercising? _____

   d. What happened to Stella's breathing rate
   after she stopped exercising? _____

   e. How long did it take for her breathing
   rate to get back to normal? _____

Once you understand how we breathe, award
yourself a star in the box.

The bones inside your body are joined together to make your **skeleton**. There are over 200 bones in your skeleton. Some of them, such as those in your ear, are very small; while others, like those in your arms and legs, are quite large.

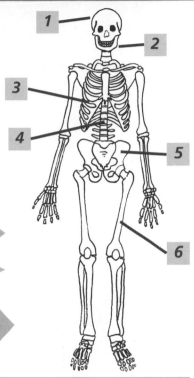

Your skeleton does three main jobs:

It supports your body and stops you from flopping over.

It helps you to move.

It protects some of your important organs. For example, the skull protects your brain and your ribs protect your lungs.

1. Which label on the above skeleton points to:

   a. skull ____   **b.** ribs ____   **c.** backbone ____
   d. jaw ____   **e.** pelvis ____   **f.** thighbone ____

2. Which of the bones labelled would be moving when:

   a. You talk **b.** You walk **c.** You breathe in deeply?

3. Not all animals have skeletons. Which of the following animals don't have skeletons?

   a. fish ____   **b.** worm ____   **c.** slug ____
   d. rabbit ____   **e.** frog ____   **f.** jellyfish ____

4. Complete this passage:

   The skull and the ribs are made of **b** _____ and form part of the **s** _____ . The **s** _____ is found in the head where it protects the **b** _____ .
   The **r** _____ are found in the **c** _____ , where they protect the **h** _____ and **l** _____ .

When you understand what your skeleton does,
award yourself a star in the box.

107

Joints connect bones together. They enable your body to move around and there are two main types:

A hinge joint, such as your knee. The joint is behind your knee cap and allows you to move your lower leg backward and forward, but not from side to side.

A ball and socket joint, such as your shoulder joint. This joint alllows you to move your arm from side to side as well as backwards and forwards.

Muscles are attached to your bones and enable you to move. Muscles work in pairs by contracting (getting shorter). When a muscle contracts it pulls on the bone it is attached to and makes it move. For example, when your bicep muscle contracts, your arm moves up and when its pair, the tricep, contracts, your arm moves down.

Bicep muscle

Tricep muscle

1. What does a joint do?

_____

2. Name one other hinge joint and one other ball and socket joint.

_____

3. What does contracting mean?

_____

4. What happens when the biceps muscle in your arm contracts?

_____

Once you know all about joints and muscles, award yourself a star in the box.

TEETH
TEST 10

Like many other animals humans have teeth to help them eat. **Teeth are part of your skeleton and they are set into your jaw bone**. As a young child you will have a total of 20 teeth, which are called baby teeth. These will gradually fall out and will be replaced by adult teeth.

You have three different types of tooth:

Incisors: the sharp, straight-edged teeth in the front of your mouth. These are used for biting into food.

Molars: the bumpy teeth at the back of your mouth. These are used for chewing or grinding food.

Canines: the sharp-teeth on the top and bottom jaw, between the incisors and molars. These are used to tear food.

Teeth are very hard, but they can be destroyed by acid. Acid is produced by tiny germs called bacteria that live in your mouth and feed on the sugar in your food. This layer of bacteria is called **plaque**. **It is important to brush and floss your teeth every day, to remove the plaque.**

1. Which types of teeth do you use for:

   a. biting?   **b.** chewing?   **c.** tearing?

2. What is plaque?

   _____

3. Which of the following could be bad for your teeth?

   a. apple juice ___ **b.** candy ___ **c.** carrots ___
   d. potatoes ___ **e.** apples ___ **f.** potato chips ___
   g. cola drink ___ **h.** chocolate ___

4. Why must you clean your teeth regularly?

   _____

5. How many baby teeth does a young child have?

   _____

Now that you know what your different teeth do, award yourself a star in the box.

109

Like all living things, humans reproduce. This means they **produce baby humans that grow up into adult humans**.

The type of reproduction found in humans is called **sexual reproduction** because it involves **two parents, one male and one female**. When a man and a woman make love, special cells called sperm are passed from the man to the woman, inside her body.

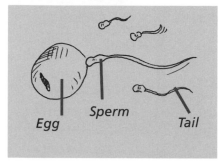

Egg   Sperm   Tail

Sometimes one of the **sperm cells** finds its way to another **special cell called an egg** in the woman's body, and the two cells join together. This is called **fertilization**.

Sperm cells have a tail so that they can swim to the egg.

When the egg and the sperm join together inside the female's body we call it **internal fertilization**. Many other animals produce babies in the same way. However, some animals use **external fertilization**. For example, when fish mate, they both release their sex cells directly into the water. The sperm from the male then swims through the water to join the female's egg. Many of the sperm don't make it and die.

---

1. What do we call the sex cells produced by:

   a. a man?   **b.** a woman?

   _____   _____

2. How are sperm cells designed for their job?

   _____

3. What does fertilization mean?

   _____

4. Fish produce many more sex cells than humans. Why do you think this is?

   _____

5. What does reproduction mean?

   _____

When you know how an egg is fertilized, award yourself a star in the box.

In a woman, once the egg and the sperm have joined together, the **fertilized egg** grows into a baby in a special place called the **uterus** or **womb**. While the baby is growing, the woman is pregnant. The baby takes nine months to grow inside its mother's body before it is ready to be born. This is called the **gestation period**. The gestation period lasts for a different length of time in different mammals.

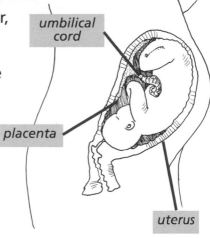

umbilical cord

placenta

uterus

While the baby is inside its mother's uterus it cannot feed itself or breathe for itself. Instead it gets all the food and oxygen it needs from its mother. Inside her body is a special organ called the **placenta**. The mother's and the baby's blood travels through the placenta and the baby's blood absorbs the things it needs to stay alive and grow through the umbilical cord. **This happens in all mammals**.

---

1. What does gestation period mean?

_____

2. Which of the following mammals do you think has the longest gestation period?

a. elephant **b.** rabbit **c.** human **d.** dog

3. Where in the mother's body does the baby grow?

a. stomach **b.** liver **c.** uterus

4. While a woman is pregnant how does the baby get the food and oxygen it needs to grow?

_____

5. Why do you think it is important for a pregnant woman to eat a good, balanced diet?

_____

Once you have correctly completed this page, award yourself a star in the box.

111

LOOKING AFTER A NEWBORN BABY
TEST 13

We all start life as a single fertilized egg cell and eventually grow up into an adult person.

We spend the first nine months of our lives growing from a single cell into a baby inside our mother's uterus.

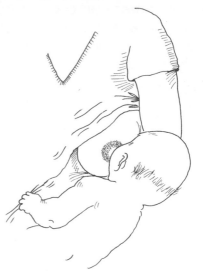

In the first few months of a baby's life, the mother feeds it with milk made specially for the baby in her breasts. All mammals produce milk for their babies. The milk contains all the important nutrients that the baby needs to grow and keep it from getting ill.

When we are born we are completely helpless, and our parents have to do everything for us. They have to feed us, clean us, keep us warm and protect us. It is also very important that we are loved, talked to and taught. This helps to develop our minds as well as our bodies.

Other animals, such as birds, also look after their babies by feeding, protecting and keeping them warm.

---

1. Give two reasons why mother's milk is the best thing for newborn babies.

    _____

2. Only mammals feed their babies with milk. Which of these animals provide milk for their babies?

    a. fish __ **b.** humans __ **c.** elephants __ **d.** birds __

3. Why do you think it is important for parents to talk to their babies?

    _____

4. A newborn baby is completely helpless. List three ways that adults must look after a baby.

    _____

Now that you know how to look after a newborn baby, award yourself a star in the box right.

From our birth to the age of 18 years we are continually **growing and getting bigger** and our **bodies and minds are changing and developing**. Many changes take place during this time.

The first three years of our life after we are born is called our **infancy. This is when we learn to walk and talk.**

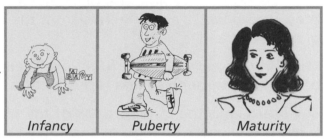

| Infancy | Puberty | Maturity |

Between the ages of 12 years and 15 years we go through another important stage, called **puberty**. (In some people puberty can occur earlier than 12 and later than 15). This is when our **bodies start to develop sexually** so that girls start to produce eggs and boys start to produce sperm.

By the time we reach 18 years, our bodies are **fully grown**, and we are said to have reached **maturity**; but our minds continue to develop for many years.

---

1. Link these important stages in our lives with the correct ages.

    1. Infancy   a. 12 – 15 years

    2. Puberty   b. 18 years

    3. Maturity   c. 0 – 3 years

2. At what age do girls and boys start to develop sexually?

    _____

3. Link the following words with their correct meaning.

    1. Reproduction   a. a gradual change in the body

    2. Growth   b. producing new human beings

    3. Development   c. a gradual increase in size.

When you understand about puberty and adulthood, award yourself a star in the box.

113

Plants have **roots**, **stems** and sometimes **flowers**.

The **roots are found in the soil**. They branch and spread out to reach as much of the soil as they can. The roots have two functions. They hold the plant down in the soil and they absorb water and minerals from the soil, which the plant needs to live.

The **flowers** have just one function. **Their job is to produce baby plants through sexual reproduction.**

The **stem links the other organs of the plant together**. It holds the leaves up high so that they can get lots of sunlight and carbon dioxide to make food; it also holds the flowers up which helps them to reproduce; and the stem also passes water and minerals from the roots to the leaves and flowers, and food from the leaves down to the roots.

---

1. Look at the picture of the plant
Which label points to:

   a. the roots?_____   **b.** a leaf?_____

   c. the stem?_____   **d.** a flower?_____

2. Which labelled part:

   a. makes food for the plant? _____
   b. transports food and water
      through the plant? _____
   c. carries out reproduction? _____
   d. absorbs water from the soil? _____

3. What are the two main functions
   of the roots?
   _____

4. Why is the stem of a plant so important?
   _____

5. What is the job of a flower?
   a. to look nice _____   **b.** to reproduce _____
   c. to make food _____

Once you have 100 per cent, award yourself a star in the box.

PLANTS MAKE FOOD
TEST 16

Plants are living things because they can grow and reproduce. Unlike animals, they do not need to eat food because they can make their own. They do this through a process known as **photosynthesis**.

Photosynthesis happens in the leaves of the plant. The leaf needs three things to make food:

Water, which it gets from the soil.	A gas called carbon dioxide, which it gets from the air.	Light energy, which it gets from the sun.

For photosynthesis to work, the plant needs to be quite warm. The food that is made in the leaf by photosynthesis is then used to give the plant energy and to help it grow and reproduce.

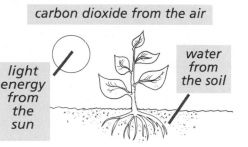

carbon dioxide from the air

light energy from the sun

water from the soil

---

1. What is photosynthesis?
   _____

2. Name 3 things a plant needs for photosynthesis.
   _____

3. Why do plants grow faster in the summer than in the winter?
   _____

4. Mr. Patel left a cardboard box on his lawn for two weeks. When he lifted it up, he found that the grass underneath was dead. Explain why this happened.
   _____

5. During photosynthesis, plants make oxygen as well as food. We can write the process of photosynthesis like a sum. Complete this:

Carbon Dioxide + (a) _____ + (b) _____
= (c) _____ + Oxygen

Once you have learned how plants make food, award yourself a star in the box.

115

Like all living things plants are able to reproduce.
To carry out sexual reproduction, plants have to make special sex cells. The male sex cells are called **pollen;** and the female sex cell is the **egg**. These are made inside the flower.

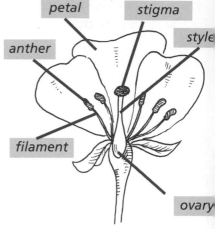

The male part of the flower is called the **stamen**. It is made up of the **anther**, which is where the pollen grains are made, and is held up by a stalk called the **filament**.

The female part of the flower is called the **carpel**. It is made up of the **style, stigma** and the **ovary**, where the eggs are made. In order for the plants to reproduce, the male pollen grains have to be moved or transferred from an anther to a carpel, usually of a different flower.

---

1. Look at these flower parts:

anther	ovary	stigma
filament	style	petals

a. Which of these parts makes up the stamen?

_____

b. What is the name of the female part of the flower?

_____

c. Where are eggs made?

_____

d. Where are pollen grains made?

_____

When you can identify all the parts of a plant, award yourself a star in the box.

When pollen is transferred from the male part of a flower to the female part of another flower, it is called **pollination.**

Pollination can happen in two ways. Some plants have brightly coloured petals, which attract insects such as bees to the flower. The pollen from one flower sticks to the bee's body, and then gets rubbed off onto the stigma of another flower, when the bee visits it.

Other flowers have small plain petals and are not attractive to insects. With these kinds of plants, the anthers and the stigma hang outside. When the wind blows it picks up pollen from one flower and carries it to another flower.

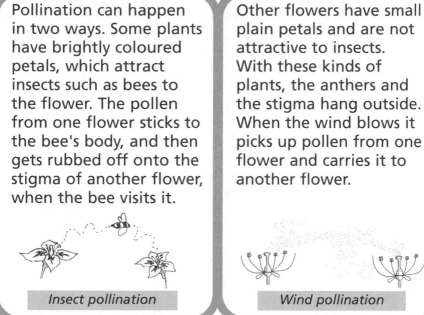

Insect pollination

Wind pollination

During pollination, pollen lands on the stigma of a flower. The pollen grain then grows down through the style into the ovary of the flower. Here it joins with an egg inside the ovary. This is called **fertilization**.

1. What does the word pollination mean?

   _____

2. Explain the difference between insect pollination and wind pollination.

   _____

3. Roses have brightly coloured petals and grass flowers have dull green petals. What does this tell us about how they transfer pollen?

   _____

4. During pollination, where on the plant does the pollen land?

   _____

Once you have understood how flowers are pollinated, award yourself a star in the box.

117

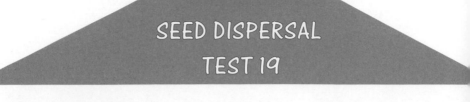

After fertilization the **egg grows into a seed** that contains a **tiny baby plant** and a **food store**.

When the seeds have grown to a certain size they have to leave the plant they are growing on, and spread out to grow on their own. The spreading out of seeds is called **dispersal**. It is important for plants to disperse their seeds. If not, the baby plants that grow from the seeds would not get enough sunlight and water, as the parent plant would get it all. This means that the baby plant would not grow properly.

Plants use different ways of dispersing their seeds. For example, the **seeds of a peach grow inside a juicy fruit**. Animals, such as humans, pick the peach and eat it, and then throw away the seed from the middle.

seed

juicy fruit

feathery parachute

seed

Dandelion seeds grow with a feathery parachute around them. The wind blows the seeds away from the parent plant. When the seed has been dispersed and lands on the ground it may start to grow.

1. What would you find inside a seed?

   _____

2. What does seed dispersal mean?

   _____

3. Maple trees produce seeds with little wing-like parts attached to them, but blackberries produce seeds inside a juicy fruit. How do you think maple seeds and blackberry seeds are dispersed?

   _____

4. What would happen to the seeds if they were not dispersed and started growing right under the parent plant?

   _____

118

If all your answers are correct, award yourself a star in the box.

When the baby plant starts to grow from the seed we say that the **seed is germinating**. For germination a seed needs **water, oxygen** and **warmth**. The baby plant uses up the food store in the seed and starts to grow. First it grows tiny roots down into the soil, and then a stem with leaves on it grows up towards the light.

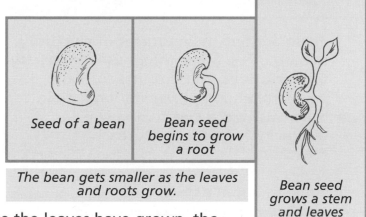

Seed of a bean

Bean seed begins to grow a root

The bean gets smaller as the leaves and roots grow.

Bean seed grows a stem and leaves

Once the leaves have grown, the baby plant is able to **photosynthesize** and can make its own food.

1. What does the word germinate mean?

   _____

2. Name three things that a seed needs to germinate.

   _____

3. Why won't seeds germinate in a refrigerator?

   _____

4. Can you think of a reason why

   a. the root of a baby plant grows downward into the soil

   _____

   but

   b. the stem and leaves grow upward?

   _____

Once you have learned all about germination, award yourself a star in the box.

119

ELECTRICITY AND CIRCUITS
TEST 21

Electricity is a type of energy that flows through certain materials. Materials that allow electricity to flow through them are called conductors.

Metals are good conductors

but most other materials are insulators because they don't allow electricity to flow through them.

There are **two main sources of electricity** in our homes. Some things use **electricity from outlets**, which comes through wires from huge power stations; while others use **batteries** that make electricity from chemicals reacting together.

Some things in **nature also produce electricity**. For example, lightning is caused by massive bolts of electricity from the clouds, and we use the electricity in our nerves to send messages around our bodies.

---

1. Is electricity a type of:

   a. force?___   **b.** energy?___   **c.** chemical reaction?___

2. Look at this list of things that use electricity in the home. Which ones use batteries and which ones use electricity from wall outlets?

   a. pocket calculator ____   **e.** bedside lamp ____
   b. desktop computer ____   **f.** flashlight ____
   c. refrigerator ____   **g.** ipod ____
   d. vacuum cleaner ____

3. Write down five things that might be found in a kitchen that use electricity.

   _____

Now you know which things use electricity and which use batteries, award yourself a star in the box.

Metal is a **conductor of electricity**. In our homes we use metal wires to carry electricity into and out of electrical appliances such as washing machines, radios and lights.

Metal is also a good **conductor of heat** and we use metals for making things like radiators and saucepans when we want heat to pass through them easily.

metal pins

plastic cover

live wires

However, although electricity and heat are very useful, they can also be very dangerous. If we touched a live metal wire (one carrying electricity), we would get an electric shock. So the electric wires in our homes are covered in plastic, as plastic is a good **electrical insulator**.

When a saucepan is used for cooking, the handle would get very hot if it was made of metal and we would burn ourselves trying to pick it up. So the handle is usually made of wood or plastic. Wood and plastic do not conduct heat as they are good **heat insulators.**

1. Divide these things into four groups—
   heat conductors, heat insulators, electrical conductors and **electrical insulators**:

   metal saucepan   wooden stick   aluminum
   paper   plastic cup   string   silver bracelet
   china plate   copper wire   iron   gold

   Heat conductors _____

   Heat insulators _____

   Electrical conductors _____

   Electrical insulators _____

2. What do we mean when we say something is:
   a. a good conductor of heat?
   b. a good insulator of electricity ?

   _____

Once you have learned about conductors and insulators, award yourself a star in the box.

121

FORCES
TEST 23

Even though we don't always realize it, **we are surrounded by forces all the time.** Some examples of forces include:

Gravity	Elastic	Friction	Upthrust
pulls everything down towards the earth	such as when you stretch a rubber band	makes it hard to rub two rough surfaces together	force of water that stops boats from sinking

A **force** can be described as a push or a pull. When forces act on an object, they can make the object:

> **move faster**   **slow down**
> **change its shape**   **change direction**

However, if two forces act on an object in **opposite directions,** they may balance out, so nothing happens. In this picture, gravity pulls down on the girl, but the chair is pushing up so she doesn't move. Gravity is pulling down on the book, but friction between the book and the girl's hands balances the gravity, so the book doesn't move.

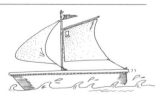

1. Which two words can be used to describe a force?

   _____   _____

2. Look at this boat on the water.

   a. Name the two forces acting on the boat.

   _____

   b. Why doesn't the boat move up or down?

   _____

   c. What would happen if gravity became greater than the upthrust?

   _____

Now you know all about forces, award yourself a star in the box.

MAGNETS
TEST 24

Magnetism is a type of force. If a magnet is placed close to some iron pins and some wooden matches, the pins will be pulled towards the magnet and will stick to it. However, the wooden matches will not move. This is because magnetism attracts only specific metals and nothing else.

> **Anything made out of iron, steel, cobalt or nickel can be attracted to a magnet.**

The two ends of a magnet are called the **poles**. One is called the **north pole** and the other the **south pole**.

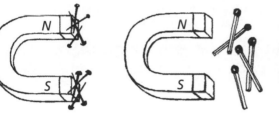

Iron pins will be attracted to either end of a magnet, but the matchsticks will be unaffected.

However, when we put two magnets together, they may be attracted to each other or they may be pushed away (repelled). **While a north pole and a south pole attract each other, two north or two south poles will repel each other.**

---

1. Is magnetism a type of:

   a. energy?___   **b.** force?___   **c.** electricity?___

2. Simon has dropped steel keys and some copper coins behind the sofa. Can he get them both out using a magnet on a string?

   _____

3. Name four types of metal that magnets attract.

   _____

4.

   | N | | S | | S | | N |

   a. Explain what will happen to the magnets (above).

   _____

   b. What will happen if one of the magnets is turned around the opposite way?

   _____

Now you know what is and isn't magnetic, award yourself a star in the box.

123

Light is a type of energy that moves from one place to another. Some things, such as the sun or a light bulb, make their own light. They are called light sources and we can see them because light from them travels into our eyes.

Most objects don't make their own light, but we can still see them because light from a light source hits the object and bounces off into our eyes.

Light travels in straight lines. This is why we see shadows. If you stand between a lamp and a wall, a dark patch (your shadow) forms on the wall where the light can't reach – because light can't travel through your body.

Light travels fastest through empty space, but it also moves through most gases, some liquids and a few solids.

If the torch is moved farther away from the object, the shadow will become smaller.

shadow

object

light source

---

1. Is light a type of:

    a. force?__ **b.** electricity ?__ **c.** energy ?__

2. Which of these objects is a light source?

    a. a flame __ **b.** a book __ **c.** a car headlight __
    d. a television __ **e.** a teapot __ **f.** the sun __

3. Complete this sentence with the correct statement from below. We can see a ball because:

    a. light from our eyes goes to the ball
    b. a ball is a light source
    c. light reflects off the ball and into our eyes

    _____

4. Why can we see through a glass window, but not through a brick wall?

    _____

Once you understand how light works, award yourself a star in the box.

If you pluck a string on a guitar, two things happen. You can **see** the string moving back and forth very quickly; we say that **the string is vibrating.**

You also **hear** a sound. **This is because the vibration of the string makes the air particles around it vibrate.** The vibrations spread out through the air and into your ear where you "**hear**" it. Unlike light, sounds can be made by all sorts of things, when they move and cause vibrations.

Sound vibrations can travel through all the things around us, whether solids, liquids or gases. As long as an object is made of particles (as every object is) the particles can vibrate back and forth. Sound travels fastest through solids and slowest through gases.

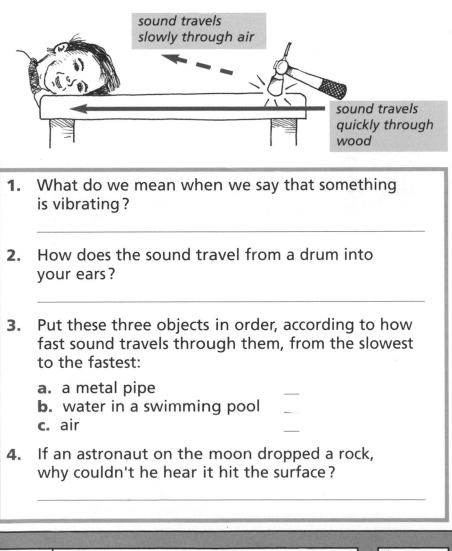

sound travels slowly through air

sound travels quickly through wood

1. What do we mean when we say that something is vibrating?

   _____

2. How does the sound travel from a drum into your ears?

   _____

3. Put these three objects in order, according to how fast sound travels through them, from the slowest to the fastest:

   a. a metal pipe   __
   b. water in a swimming pool   __
   c. air   __

4. If an astronaut on the moon dropped a rock, why couldn't he hear it hit the surface?

   _____

Once you know where sound comes from, award yourself a star in the box.

125

Everything around us can be described as either a solid, a liquid or a gas. For example, the air is a gas; water is a liquid; and tables and paper are solids.

| The steam from a kettle is a gas | Cooking oil is a liquid | A brick is a solid |

Some things, such as water, can change easily from solid to liquid, from liquid to gas and back again.

| Solid water is called ice | Liquid water is just called water | Water as a gas is called steam or water vapour. |

The main difference between solids, liquids and gases is the amount of heat energy they have. If you heat a lump of ice it turns into water; and if you heat water in a saucepan it turns into steam. On the other hand, water placed in a freezer will lose heat and turn to ice.

1. Divide these things into solids, liquids and gases.

> water vapour   orange juice
> oxygen   wood   blood   glass
> ice   carbon dioxide

Solids	Liquids	Gases
_____	_____	_____

2. What happens to steam when it cools down?

_____

3. Link these words to their meanings:

1. melting   **a.** changing from a liquid to a gas

2. freezing   **b.** changing from a solid to a liquid

3. evaporating   **c.** changing from a liquid to a solid

Now you know the difference between solids, liquids and gases, award yourself a star in the box, right.

The things around us are made up of different **materials.**
For example, **some things are made of wood, some are
made of metal and others are made of plastic, glass, paper,
cloth** and so on.

**Different materials are used because of their
different properties.** There are many different properties,
which include **hardness, softness, strength or flexibility,**
and you would choose your material according to what you
needed your object for.

For example, **aluminum and iron are both types of metal.**
They are both very **hard and strong,** but they also have
 other very different properties and are
used for different things.
Aluminum is used for
making airplanes, because it is much
lighter than iron. Cars are made out of iron
because it is stronger than aluminum.

1. Match these materials with their properties

Materials	Properties
Wood	Brittle
Clingwrap	Hard
Glass	Strong
Metal	Flexible
Cloth	Waterproof

2. Link these properties with their meanings

1. flexible   a. light passes through it
2. magnetic   b. does not break easily
3. strong   c. can be bent easily
4. brittle   d. easy to break or snap
5. transparent   e. attracted to magnets

3. Why do cars use liquid gasoline and not solid coal
   as fuel ? Choose one of the following statements:

   a. Liquids weigh less than solids

   b. Liquids are cheaper than solids

   c. Liquids flow and solids do not

Now you know how to choose the right material,
award yourself a star in the box, left.

127

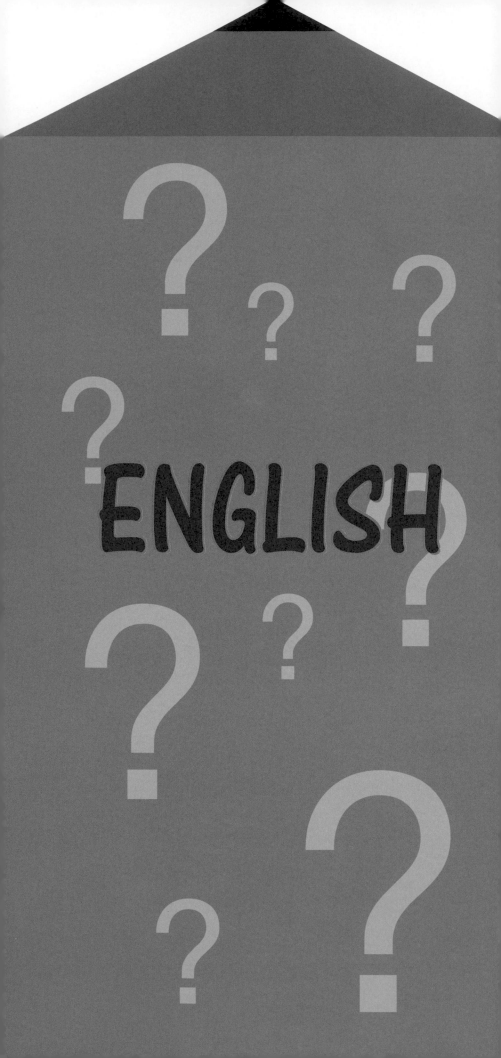

SPELLING
GETTING IT RIGHT

It is important to spell correctly. After all, if you don't, there could be a lot of misunderstandings. Some of these might be quite funny. What would happen, for example, if you wrote to a store, returning some shoes that had fallen apart on the first day you wore them? You might ask in the letter for a new **pear**. If you did this, they would send you some fruit, not shoes! The word for a kind of fruit is spelled *pear;* but the word for two of anything, although we say it in the same way, is spelled *pair*!

There are quite a few words in English that sound the same but have different meanings and are spelled differently, as you will discover as you work through this book.

If you are not sure how to spell a word or what its meaning is, you can always look it up in a dictionary. But in order to look up a word, you need to know your alphabet. This is because all the words in a dictionary are in alphabetical order.

Once you have read this page, award yourself a star in the box, left.

129

Here is the alphabet. Make sure you can say it perfectly without looking, and get someone to test you. (Even if you have a parent who does not speak English very well, he or she can learn with you.)

A B C D E F G H I J K L M N O P Q R S T U V W X Y Z

If you want to look up the word "DOME", for example, first find the **D**s in the dictionary. They will be after **C**, of course, and before **E**. Then look for the words that begin DO, then DOM, and finally DOME. (The meaning of this word is something that is shaped like half a sphere.)

Once you have learned the alphabet, award yourself a star in the box, right.

TEST 1

Can you put the words below in alphabetical order?

jam	orange
dog	X-ray
loud	cheese
mat	read
queen	nail
zoo	van
ball	skin
under	easy
ape	wedding
piano	frog
town	kettle
heel	yellow
grass	igloo

Once you have successfully completed this page, award yourself a star in the box, left.

131

TEST 2

The words in the box below all begin with S. Can you put them in alphabetical order? Remember: as they all begin with S, you will need to put them in order according to the second letter. If you find several words with the same *second* letter, these words will then have to go in order according to the third letter, or maybe even the fourth letter.

To help you begin, put the word SALAD first. It begins with SA, but so does SANDWICH. The third letter in SALAD is L. The letter L comes before the letter N, which is the third letter in the word SANDWICH. You will know this if you can say your alphabet well.

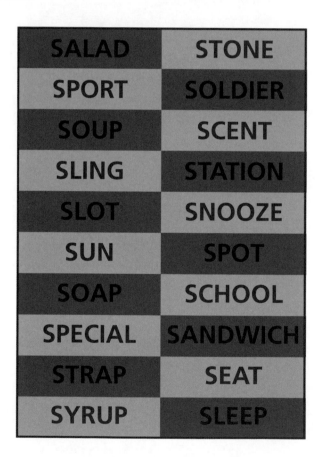

SALAD	STONE
SPORT	SOLDIER
SOUP	SCENT
SLING	STATION
SLOT	SNOOZE
SUN	SPOT
SOAP	SCHOOL
SPECIAL	SANDWICH
STRAP	SEAT
SYRUP	SLEEP

Once you have successfully completed this page, award yourself a star in the box, right.

The children in this list below are all in the same class. The teacher has to put their names in the register but needs some help. Can you assist her, please?

The names need to go in alphabetical order, according to the children's surnames. This means that **James Brown** will come somewhere before **Sarah Glass** in the register because **B** for **Brown** comes before **G** for **Glass**. If two surnames begin with the same letter, you will need to put them in order according to the second letter. Please write out the entire class register.

Alice Thompson	Jenny Andrews
Andrew Dubois	Amber Kim
Sarah Glass	Frank Kent
Karen Simons	Alison Turner
Donna Patel	Paul Yee
James Brown	Robert Marks
Emily Parsons	Steven Allsop
Jason Smith	Keesha Johnson
Michael Dixon	Reem Mahdi
Rosie Mitchell	Luke Dougall
Brian Gross	Anna Storr

Once you have got this test completely correct, award yourself a star in the box, left.

133

TEST 4

Below you will find some empty boxes. These stand for missing letters that you have to try to find. There are 4 missing letters, with one box for each, in every row. So each missing word has 4 letters. To the left of each row of boxes, you will find a clue. Read the clue and then write out the missing word with the correct spelling. One more thing: as you go down the line of missing words, the words change by just one letter each time. That's how you can check if you have the right word.

On your marks, get set, start *now*!

1. **Your fingers are part of this, and you have a left one and a right one.** ☐ ☐ ☐ ☐

2. **Found on a beach** ☐ ☐ ☐ ☐

3. **To mail** ☐ ☐ ☐ ☐

4. **To loan** ☐ ☐ ☐ ☐

5. **To fold** ☐ ☐ ☐ ☐

6. **Part of a necklace** ☐ ☐ ☐ ☐

7. **At the top of your body** ☐ ☐ ☐ ☐

8. **To listen** ☐ ☐ ☐ ☐

9. **An animal** ☐ ☐ ☐ ☐

10. **Close by** ☐ ☐ ☐ ☐

Once you have successfully completed this page, award yourself a star in the box, right.

Can you guess what the missing words are and spell them correctly? To help, we have given you the first letter of each missing word. The number of dashes shows the number of letters that are missing from each word.

Jessica felt very c _ _ _ and was shivering, so her mother said she should go to b _ _ with a h _ _ water bottle. She would probably feel b _ _ _ _ _ in the morning. Jessica s _ _ _ _ very well that night.

Tyler had some new hockey s _ _ _ _ _. He was very p _ _ _ _ of them and could not wait to w _ _ _ them for the first t _ _ _. Perhaps they would help him score a g _ _ _.

Once you have got this test completely correct, award yourself a star in the box, left.

135

Perhaps you have sometimes seen these two letters **Q** and **U** together when you are reading. When they are written side by side, they sound like **KW**. Can you spell the following missing words?

1. In some video games, players go on a _ _ _ _ _.

2. The girl is good at sports and runs very _ _ _ _ _ _ _.

3. A half of a half is a _ _ _ _ _ _ _ _.

4. It is so _ _ _ _ _ that I cannot hear a sound.

5. Can you _ _ _ _ _ like a duck?

6. The boy asked his teacher a _ _ _ _ _ _ _ _ _.

Once you have successfully completed this page, award yourself a star in the box, right.

You may have seen **W** and **R** together sometimes, too. If they come together at the beginning of a word, you do not say the **W**. It is silent. You just say **R**. All of the following missing words below contain the letters **WR**.

1. I promised to _ _ _ _ _ to my friend when I moved.

2. If something is wet, you need to _ _ _ _ _ out the water.

3. If something is not right it is _ _ _ _ _ .

4. The joint between your hand and your arm is your _ _ _ _ _ .

5. Jeff was always _ _ _ _ _ _ _ _ _ _ and moving about in his seat.

6. The bridge wore a _ _ _ _ _ _ of flowers.

Once you have successfully completed this page, award yourself a star in the box, left.

137

When the letters **K** and **N** come together at the beginning of a word, the **K** is always silent. You just say the **N**. All the missing words below start with **KN**, as you can see. Can you guess what they are and spell them correctly?

---

1. To tie up string   KN _ _

2. To put your knees on the floor   KN _ _ _

3. Parts of your fingers   KN _ _ _ _ _ _

4. To make something out of wool   KN _ _

5. To bang at a door   KN _ _ _

When the letters **P** and **H** come together, you say this as **F**. In the sentences below, there are missing words that all have **PH** in them somewhere, pronounced as **F**. Can you spell these words, writing them correctly?

---

6. She took some very good
   p _ _ _ _ _ _ _ _ _ _ _ with her camera.

7. She wanted the movie star's
   _ _ _ _ _ _ _ _ _ _ and so asked him to
   sign his name.

8. Another name for a druggist is
   a _ _ _ _ _ _ _ _ _ _ _.

9. Do you talk on the   _ _ _ _ _ _ _ _ _ _ ?

138

Here is a very useful golden rule to help with spelling. You usually put **I** before **E** except after **C**. Repeat that: *I before E except after* **C**. Now that you know this, choose from the spellings in brackets and write down the word correctly.

1. We (*received/recieved*) the parcel yesterday.

2. The (*thief/theif*) stole the cash.

3. I (*believe/beleive*) they have gone to France.

4. The fire (*cheif/chief*) reminded people to check their smoke detectors regularly.

5. The old lady wept in (*grief/greif*).

6. The meeting was very (*breif/brief*) and did not last long.

7. After an earthquake, airplanes deliver (*releif/relief*) supplies.

But there are some exceptions! In each of the following sentences, the right answer breaks the rule. Now that you know this, see if you can spell the three words correctly.

8. He was the (*heir/hier*) to the throne.

9. (*Their/thier*) holiday plans look very exciting.

10. He (*seized/siezed*) her by the arm and helped the blind lady across the road.

Once you have successfully completed this page, award yourself a star in the box, left.

139

Each of the words that you have to find has a letter in it that is silent. Try to guess what each word is. When you write it down, underline the silent letter.

1. **To write your name at the end of a letter or on a cheque.**

2. **You use this to tidy your hair.**

3. **A bicycle has two of these, and a tricycle has three.**

4. **Your arm or leg.**

5. **The joint halfway down your leg.**

6. **Two halves make this.**

7. **A spooky figure.**

8. **A statue found in gardens.**

9. **To eat away at something.**

10. **A tool used in fixing cars.**

Now try this. Can you spell the words with the missing letters? They all end in **H**. The dashes show the number of missing letters, and we have provided clues.

11. **To make a noise in your throat when you have a cold C _ _ H**

12. **To make a noise when you hear something funny L _ _ _ H**

13. **To throw a baseball P _ _ _ H**

14. **To hurry R _ _ H**

Once you have got this test completely correct, award yourself a star in the box, right.

Read through the following sentences out loud. You will see that they contain words that sound the same but that are spelled differently and have very different meanings.

Most dogs have a *tail*.
The *Tale* of Peter Rabbit is a very charming story.

People sing a *hymn* when they go to church.
She gave *him* a book for his birthday.

She began to *pour* the lemonade from the jug.
Each of the tiny holes in your skin that helps it to breathe is called a *pore*.

The material was *plain* and had no pattern.
They travelled to Africa by *plane*.

You should not *steal* other people's property.
Steel is a very strong metal.

She is very *vain* and always looks in the mirror.
Each *vein* carries blood through your body.

The *story* was very exciting.
Peter lives in a thirty-*storey* building.

In Elizabethan times, people wore a fancy collar called a *ruff*.
Jared thought the gang were very *rough*.

Once you have studied the above sentences, award yourself a star in the box, left.

141

Please write out each sentence below, choosing the correct spelling from the two meanings in brackets so that the sentence makes sense.

1. Would you like a (*piece/peace*) of this delicious cake?

2. The boys went for a walk together along the (*peer/pier*).

3. The woods were full of white-tailed (*deer/dear*) .

4. How many (*tears/tiers*) are there on that wedding cake?

5. A (*dough/doe*) is the mother of a fawn.

6. One of my favourite herbs is (*thyme/time*).

7. Who (*knows/nose*) the right answer?

8. You (*knead/need*) nerves of (*steal/steel*) to look down from a skyscraper building.

9. I (*mist/missed*) you when you were away on holiday.

10. You have probably (*groan/grown*) a lot in the last year.

11. Have you (*scene/seen*) your next door neighbours today?

12. Have you (*heard/herd*) the news?

13. It is about to (*teem/team*) with rain.

14. The boy (*caught/cot*) chickenpox.

Once you can complete this test within 60 seconds award yourself a star in the box, right.

If there is more than one of anything, we have to change it from a singular to a plural and usually do this by adding **S**. So we have one orange but two orange**s**; one ship but three ship**s**, one shoe but two shoe**s**.

When a word ends in **Y**, however, if we turn it into a plural we usually take away the **Y** and add **IES**. The plural of puppy is therefore puppies; and the plural of curry is curries. But if the word ends in **EY**, you keep the **EY** and just add an **S**. So the plural of chimney is chimneys; and the plural of monkey is monkeys. You will not find this hard to remember once you get some practice.

Now write out each sentence below, choosing the correct spelling from inside the brackets. A few more difficult ones have been included.
Clues: the plural of tomato is tomatoes, the plural of glass is glasses, the plural of fireman is firemen, and the plural of inch is inches. A few words even stay the same in the plural.

---

1. Alex and Hazel have visited four (*countrys/countries*) this year.

2. Do you like (*potatos/potatoes*)?

3. Newborn (*babys/babies*) are very cute.

4. There are three (*librarys/libraries*) in this town.

5. How many (*classs/classes*) are there in this school?

6. Lots of (*Scotsmans/Scotsmen*) like to wear kilts.

7. That shop sells shoes for (*ladys/ladies*) only.

8. There were seven (*sheeps/sheep*) in the field.

Once you have successfully completed this page, award yourself a star in the box, left.

143

Can you find 10 different types of fruit in the word square below? The letters can read across or down. Look carefully and be sure to list words that are spelled correctly.

G	L	X	B	C	H	E	R	R	Y
I	P	E	A	C	H	O	A	M	O
F	I	G	N	S	I	R	G	A	M
C	G	R	A	Y	P	A	R	N	E
H	Z	B	A	N	A	N	A	G	L
E	P	E	A	R	P	G	P	O	O
R	A	B	A	P	L	E	E	O	N
R	I	D	R	Z	P	E	E	R	O
Y	R	Q	A	P	P	L	E	X	N
P	L	U	M	T	P	E	E	C	H

Here is another word square. This time it contains the names of 10 countries. Can you find them all?

W	I	T	A	L	Y	C	U	L	A
A	R	G	U	N	T	F	J	C	R
L	E	G	Y	P	T	R	U	A	U
E	S	S	I	S	P	A	I	N	S
S	C	O	T	L	A	N	D	A	S
Z	O	L	P	I	C	S	D	D	I
P	O	L	A	N	D	S	S	A	A
O	R	T	E	B	R	A	Z	I	L
L	E	R	T	O	P	R	I	N	O
E	N	G	L	A	N	D	O	L	G

Once you have found all the hidden words, award yourself a star in the box, right.

TEST 14

Read through the following two stories and try to find the 10 spelling mistakes that there are in each. Write out these words, spelled in the right way, of course.

Mrs. Johnson was busy wedding in the garden. She loved to look after her plants and did so very carefully. Each Wenesday she wood spend the hole afternoon out their, pruning her rows bush or tidying the boarders. She really deserved a meddle for the glorious display. She loved two show her visitors the flours.

Sarah was looking forward to going too the disco. Lots of her freinds wood be there, and she could where her knew shoes. They where plane black with a read stripe. She hopped that Jorge would dance with her. She thought that he was grate!

Once you have successfully completed this page, award yourself a star in the box, left.

145

TAKE A

**You have been working hard at all
the tests so far, so it's time now for some fun.**

The ends of the words below are either ABLE or IBLE.
Do you know which is correct in each case?

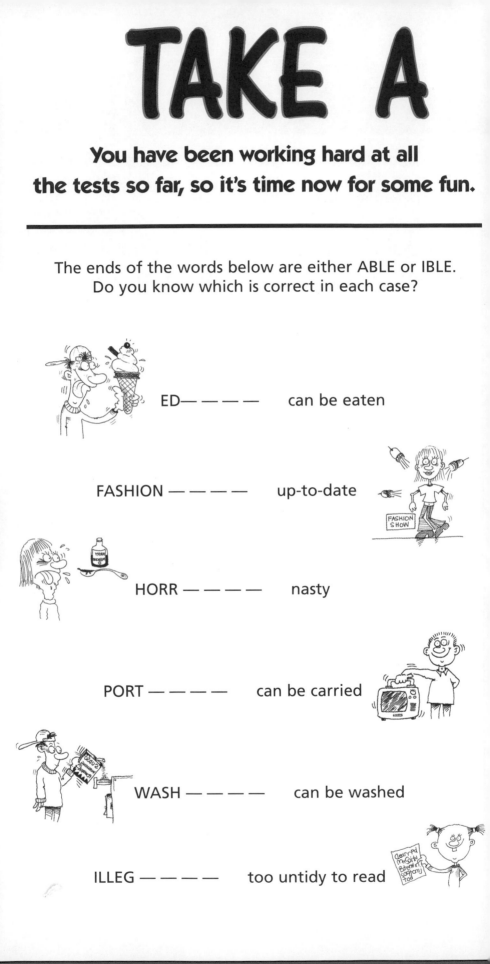

ED— — — —   can be eaten

FASHION — — — —   up-to-date

HORR — — — —   nasty

PORT — — — —   can be carried

WASH — — — —   can be washed

ILLEG — — — —   too untidy to read

BREAK

All the practice you are getting in spelling should help you with these.

Kaoru has to try to match up the fish in pairs so that the words on them rhyme. Can you help her?

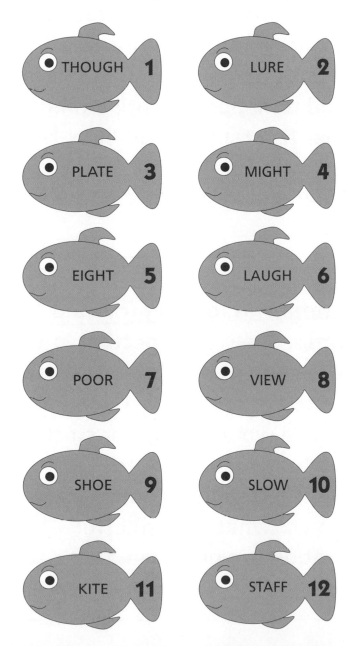

THOUGH **1**

LURE **2**

PLATE **3**

MIGHT **4**

EIGHT **5**

LAUGH **6**

POOR **7**

VIEW **8**

SHOE **9**

SLOW **10**

KITE **11**

STAFF **12**

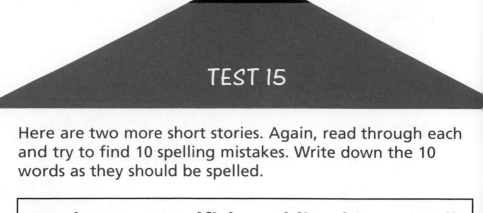

Here are two more short stories. Again, read through each and try to find 10 spelling mistakes. Write down the 10 words as they should be spelled.

Fred was a goalfish and lived in a small pond. Usually he was purrfectly happy but sometimes he got board. He would swim backwords and forwords all the time, but otherwise nothing much seamed to happen – until won day another fish came to join him. Now the too of them could swim about together and enjoy the fine whether. Life was better as a pear!

Samantha was looking forward to Chrismas. She was expecting lots of presence and new that Santa Claus would come down the chimny to bring them. She would hang her stocking at the bottom of the bed, to. They would have turky for dinner, with potatos and corrn. What a wonderful celebration it would bee, that's for shore!

Once you can complete this test within 60 seconds award yourself a star in the box, right.

TEST 16

Can you unscramble the words below? In each case, you have a clue that tells you the meaning of the word. Here are some tips. If you see the letter **Y**, chances are that it is at the end of the unscrambled word.

Copy the scrambled words into your notebook. Then check to see if your answer is right by crossing out each letter to make sure you have used them all to make the unscrambled word. It sometimes helps when unscrambling words to try each letter in turn as the possible first letter of the word.

1. Taken with a camera S P R P S H G O O H T A

2. Cross GYARN

3. Flying insect T F B Y T U E R L

4. Musical instrument R A U G T I

5. Sport T B O L A F O L

6. Food P I G T A H E S T

7. Leader of an army L L N O C O E

8. Group of musicians R C A S O H T R E

9. Lack of rain G U T D H O R

10. A drink D N O L A M E E

11. Strange Y A R R R N A X O T D E I

12. Mineral O Z R B N E

13. Planet R U E P I T J

Once you have successfully completed this page, award yourself a star in the box, left.

149

All the words you need to find this time end in **SION** or **TION** which we say as **SHUN**. Can you spell them correctly?

---

1. TV

2. You can catch a train here

3. Something that you rub on your hands

4. You get this if you eat too fast

5. A story or something that is not true, beginning with F

6. Details about something, beginning with I

7. The end of a journey, beginning with D

8. Your sight, beginning with V

9. A large house, beginning with M

10. Something a witch brews up in her cauldron, beginning with P

11. A slice or serving, beginning with P

12. Senior citizens get this money, beginning with P

13. A warning, beginning with C

14. Movement, beginning with M

Once you have got this test completely correct, award yourself a star in the box, right.

One of the best ways to practise your spelling is to ask someone to read a paragraph to you slowly and to write it down. This is called dictation. It is a good idea to ask someone in your family to read about 10 lines from a newspaper or book to you once every week. You could try the following paragraph to start with. Whoever is reading it should tell you where the commas, periods, question marks or other punctuation come.

> **When Kim went to work in New York, she could not find any suitable accommodation, so she decided to stay with her aunt, who had written to say she would be welcome. She caught the bus from the station and soon arrived. It was a large house with a red front door. Kim knocked, waited for three minutes, and then looked through the letterbox. Her aunt was out. Kim did not have a key and so could not let herself in. Kim was worried. What should she do?**

Once you have successfully completed this page, award yourself a star in the box, left.

151

TEST 18

All the words that you need to find for this exercise are spelled with the letters **OAR**, **OR** or **AW** in them somewhere. Can you guess what the words must be and spell them without any mistakes? Have a try!

1. A type of wild pig that begins with B

2. Uncooked, beginning with R

3. To make a loud sound, again beginning with R

4. You row with this, beginning with O

5. Extra, beginning with M

6. Something used to cut wood, beginning with S

7. To sketch with a pencil, beginning with D

8. There are some of these in a filing cabinet, beginning with D.

9. A fishing ship, beginning with T

10. The centre of an apple, beginning with C

11. Someone who keeps on repeating a story, beginning with B

12. To fly through the air, beginning with S

13. An irritating wound, beginning with S

14. Fright, beginning with T

15. The start of the day, beginning with D

Once you can complete this test within 60 seconds award yourself a star in the box, right.

PRACTICE MAKES PERFECT

Some words are harder to spell than others, and even adults sometimes get them wrong! That is why, if you learn to spell all the words printed here, you will really shine! If any words are new to you, and some are sure to be, use a dictionary to find out what they mean. You can also ask someone in your family how to say the words if you are not confident about them. Get someone to test you on these every day for the next week. You will probably know most of them by the end of the week.

GRATEFUL	POISON
GOLDFISH	OPPOSITE
FRIGHT	QUARREL
SAUCE	WONDER
HAPPINESS	BOISTEROUS
OXYGEN	FLANNEL
WHISTLE	FASTEN
TOUR	HANDBAG
LUGGAGE	BREAKFAST
DAZZLE	TREASURE
BUOY	FIERCE
LEISURE	EITHER
STALK	MAGICIAN
DELIGHT	PANDA
LISTEN	SPEECH
MUSCLE	SCHOOL
QUAY	SPEAK

Once you have successfully studied this page, award yourself a star in the box, left.

153

Some words have double letters in them – that is, two of the same letter next to each other. Examples are ADD, OFFER, AGREE and SOON. *Below*, you will find some clues and the first letter of each word we are looking for. The dashes again show the number of missing letters. Can you think what the words with double letters must be and spell them correctly?

1. A round container for biscuits or beer B _ _ _ _ _

2. Details of where you live A _ _ _ _ _ _ _

3. Something to spread on bread B _ _ _ _ _

4. Untidy M _ _ _ _

5. The top of a building R _ _ _

6. Not vacant O _ _ _ _ _ _ _

7. Suitcases L _ _ _ _ _ _

8. To speak or get in touch C _ _ _ _ _ _ _ _ _ _

9. A sort of meat B _ _ _

10. A crash A _ _ _ _ _ _ _

GETTING IT RIGHT AGAIN

Listed below are some more of the most commonly misspelled words. Again, if you do not know the meaning of any of them, look them up in a dictionary or ask an adult. You can always ask someone to help you say them, too. You really deserve a star if you can learn to spell them all.

WEDNESDAY	MISSISSIPPI
HANDKERCHIEF	DOUBT
ALTHOUGH	QUARREL
SOLEMN	APPRECIATE
COUGH	ACCOMMODATION
OCEAN	PLEASANT
TOUGH	RHYME
PORRIDGE	HARASS
TUESDAY	SURGEON
LLAMA	MONDAY
RECEIVE	ALMOND
SECRETARY	SEPARATE
YACHT	PIGEON
GNOME	ANTARCTIC
QUARRELLED	RHYTHM
EMBARRASS	SATELLITE
FEBRUARY	IRON
THUMB	SWORD
REFRIGERATOR	MACHINE
AMBULANCE	SENTENCE
LIAR	SINCERELY
XYLOPHONE	PRECIOUS

Once you have learned the words on this page, award yourself a star in the box, left.

155

TEST 20

This time, each group of sentences contains words that begin with the same two letters. Again, the number of dashes shows how many letters there are in the words you have to find and spell correctly.

1. _ _ _ _ _ blind mice, see how they run!
Bobby _ _ _ _ _ the ball to Joe.
The mailman shoved the envelopes _ _ _ _ _ _ _ _ the mail slot.

2. The _ _ _ _ is a pretty bird that swims.
Sugar is very _ _ _ _ _ _ .
A _ _ _ _ _ _ is used in the sport of fencing.

3. _ _ _ _ _ _ are you going for your holiday?
Please let me know _ _ _ _ _ _ _ you are coming to the party.
_ _ _ _ is the time, please?

4. What was the _ _ _ _ _ _ of last night's hockey game?
Alberta has beautiful mountain _ _ _ _ _ _ _ _ .

5. Do you _ _ _ _ that girl in the red dress?
Could you help me untie this _ _ _ _ ?
John fell over and skinned his left _ _ _ _ _ .
When a baker makes bread, he _ _ _ _ _ _ _ the dough.

6. The pirates stole a _ _ _ _ _ _ _ _ _ chest.
If at first you don't succeed, be sure to _ _ _, _ _ _ again.
The boy _ _ _ _ _ _ over the loose patio stone.

7. _ _ _ _ _ _ is an expensive cut of meat.
A wasp might _ _ _ _ _ _ you if you disturb it.
_ _ _ _ is the opposite of start.
If criminals reform, they decide to go _ _ _ _ _ _ _ _ _ .
A pig lives in a _ _ _ _ .

What a great gift we have, the gift of speech!

We can **speak** and make ourselves understood with it; we can **write** it down on paper or on a computer screen and send it thousands of miles. We can say anything we like – from the simplest thing like a shopping list to the deepest and most profound idea from deep within our minds and hearts.

When we talk or write, we do so in sentences. Each sentence is a unit by itself. A sentence can be very short and simple or long and complicated, and there are rules that govern how the words are used and positioned. These rules are the rules of grammar.

The first rule of grammar is that a sentence should make complete sense standing alone.

Here are some sentences. After each sentence say whether it is **complete** or **incomplete**.
Check your answer.

1. On Saturday we were enjoying Natalie's party.

   _____

2. Suddenly a loud crash next door _____

3. To see what had happened _____

4. The birthday cake had disappeared. _____

5. Jim, the dog, the plate off the table _____

6. He ran off with the cake ! _____

7. Rushed after him _____

Once you have completed this page, award yourself a star in the box, left.

157

22 These sentences are not complete. Using the words in the list, fill in the gap in each sentence which will make it whole:

fell   gathered   shone   beach   car

1. The summer sun _____ in the blue sky.

2. The dark rain clouds _____ over the hills.

3. The autumn leaves _____ to the ground.

4. The _____ sped down the road.

5. The waves of the sea rolled onto the _____.

23 In the box write the letter of the sentence-ending that matches the numbered sentence.

1. **Midas was a very rich king**   ☐

2. **He was told that he could have**   ☐

3. **He chose that everything he could touch**   ☐

4. **He touched the flowers**   ☐

5. **Unfortunately he touched his daughter**   ☐

6. **When his daughter turned to gold**   ☐

7. **In the end she was turned back**   ☐

Sentence endings
a. anything he wanted.
b. and she turned to gold.
c. he was very upset.
d. from gold into a live person.
e. but he always wanted more.
f. should turn to gold.
g. and they turned to gold.

When you have completed these sentences, award yourself a star in the box, right.

When we speak we use different types of sentences.
Here are four of them:

**statements   questions
commands   exclamations**

**A statement tells you
something.**
Example:
The sun is shining today.

**A command instructs
or orders something.**
Example:
Sit down at once!

**A question asks
something.**
Example:
What time is it?

**An exclamation expresses
a strong feeling.**
Example:
How amazing!

Here are seven sentences that make up a story.
Write down in the space provided what type of sentence
each one is: a **statement**, a **question** a **command** or an
exclamation.

1. The man went through
   the gate into the field,
   ignoring the large notice.

   _____

2. Dangerous bull, keep
   out!

   _____

3. Halfway across, the man
   saw the angry bull
   starting to move toward
   him.

   _____

4. The huge bull chased
   the man all over the field.

   _____

5. How terrifying!

   _____

6. The man leaped over
   the fence right into
   the duckpond.

   _____

7. What happened then?

   _____

When you have got 100 per cent,
award yourself a star in the box, left.

159

PUNCTUATING SENTENCES
TEST 25

All sentences begin with a capital letter.

All sentences end with:

a period	or	question mark	or	exclamation point
.		?		!

statements usually end with a period.
questions always end with a question mark.
commands often end with an exclamation point.
exclamations always end with an exclamation point.

An exclamation point expresses a strong feeling.
Examples:
He is completely crazy!
She took one look at the approaching tonrado and ran!
Look out!

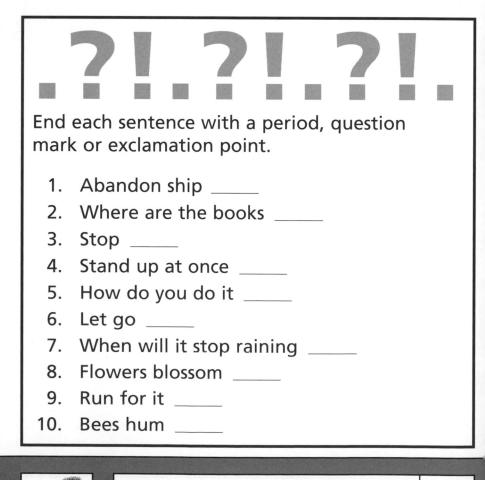

End each sentence with a period, question mark or exclamation point.

1. Abandon ship _____
2. Where are the books _____
3. Stop _____
4. Stand up at once _____
5. How do you do it _____
6. Let go _____
7. When will it stop raining _____
8. Flowers blossom _____
9. Run for it _____
10. Bees hum _____

Once you have completed this page, award yourself a star in the box, right.

A noun is a name

Every object, person, place and idea has a name.
It is through names that everything is stored in mind ready
to be used whenever that name is spoken.

Here's an example: If I say the word "sea," into your
mind comes all the knowledge of what the sea is and the
experiences you have had of it from your life, or books
or films or other people, come into your mind.

We have to use names for things if we are to show the
difference between one thing and another. If you go into
a candy store you may have a choice of a hundred different
types of chocolate bars all with slightly different tastes. You
have to know the name of the bar you want. Without a
name, you could not get exactly what you wanted.

These are names of things that you can see, touch, smell,
hear and feel, such as:

table	chair	road	playground
football	flower	sky	doll

From these sentences pick out the **common nouns**:

1. The sun shone on the sea.

   _____   _____

2. Watch the birds flying over the river.

   _____   _____

3. The boat sailed around the rock.

   _____   _____

4. She took an apple and a pear.

   _____   _____

5. I love chocolates and ice cream.

   _____   _____

Once you have learned your nouns,
award yourself a star in the box, left.

161

Every person has his or her own or proper name.

Imagine how difficult it would be if no one in your class had a name. In the same way, towns and homes have their own particular names, and so do rivers, mountains, deserts, and so on.

A **proper noun**
is the
particular name
of a
person, place or thing.

These are names of people, places and calendar dates you should know:

Brian	Diane
Claude	Toula
London	Saskatoon
France	Mexico
Monday	September

TIP BOX
All proper names start with a capital letter
e.g. **France**, **Anne**

Pick out the **proper nouns** in these sentences:

1. Alex and Sarah have gone to Winnipeg.

   _____
   _____
   _____

2. The police caught the two criminals, Smith and Jones, and took them to the station in Montreal.

   _____
   _____
   _____

3. When Paris stole the beautiful Helen from Sparta, Menelaus went to war with Troy.

   _____
   _____
   _____
   _____

4. Hannah took her cat, Tom, to the vet in Windsor.

   _____
   _____
   _____

Once you have understood proper nouns, award yourself a star in the box, right.

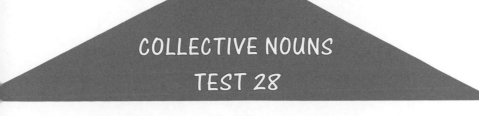

Collective nouns are groups of the same type of noun:

Examples:

a **flock** of sheep

a **herd** of cows

an **army** of soldiers

a **gaggle** of geese

a **pride** of lions

a **cluster** of diamonds

Pick out the **collective nouns** in these sentences:

1. The flock of seabirds wheeled and headed towards the shoal of fish.

   _____   _____

2. The Vikings came in their fleets of ships and behaved no better than a gang of thieves and cutthroats.

   _____   _____

3. Out of the forests of dense trees appeared a pack of wolves chasing a moose.

   _____   _____

Once you have correctly completed this page, award yourself a star in the box, left.

163

Singular means **one**.

Plural means
more than one.

Examples:

> **The book is on the shelf.**
> The word **book** is singular because there is only one.

> **The books are on the shelf.**
> The word **books** is plural because there are more than one.

Say if each word is singular or plural.

1. window _____

2. men _____

3. glasses _____

4. tree _____

5. pictures _____

We know that most nouns become plural by adding – **s**.

Make these nouns plural
Add – **s**

Singular	Plural
1. flower	_____
2. table	_____
3. piano	_____
4. house	_____

However there are many exceptions to this rule.

Add – **es**

5. potato	_____
6. tomato	_____

Change **y** to **i** and add – **es**

Singular	Plural
7. country	_____
8. reply	_____
9. sky	_____

Add – **es**

10. bus	_____
11. dish	_____
12. match	_____

Change **f** to **v** and add – **es**

13. half	_____
14. leaf	_____
15. shelf	_____

No change in plural. Can you think of one more example?

16. trout	trout
sheep	sheep
?	_____

Once you have learned your plurals,
award yourself a star in the box, right.

FIRST REVISION TEST
TESTS 31, 32, 33

31 Say whether these sentences are **complete** or **incomplete**:

1. Lucy shouted down the stairs. _____

2. The train arriving at platform four _____

3. The car down the steep hill _____

4. The mother cat had six little kittens. _____

---

32 Fill in the missing punctuation at the end of the sentence and then say whether each **sentence** is a **statement**, a **question** or a **command**.

1. Go and never return ___ _____

2. Why does the tide rise and fall ___ _____

3. It is the pull of the moon that makes the tide rise and fall ___ _____

4. Glue the mast to the frame of the model boat ___ _____

---

33 Here is the first part of a story about the Trojan War. Read it carefully and then answer the questions at the bottom.

Long, long ago there was a <u>king</u> called <u>Menelaus</u> of <u>Sparta</u>. He had a <u>wife</u> called <u>Helen</u> who was the most beautiful <u>woman</u> in all the world. Her eyes shone like a <u>cluster</u> of <u>diamonds</u> and around her <u>neck</u> hung a <u>string</u> of pearls.

From the underlined words pick out:

1. three **proper nouns**:

_____ _____ _____

2. two **collective nouns**:

_____ _____

3. five **common nouns**:

_____ _____ _____

_____ _____

If all your tests are correct, award yourself a star in the box, left.

165

VERBS
TEST 34

A noun is known as a **part of speech**. There are in fact **eight** parts of speech, and the noun is one of the most important. In the last section we learned that nouns are the names of all things. The next part of speech is a **verb**.

A **verb** expresses the **action** in the sentence.

A sentence tells us about an action, however simple it may be, and in fact every sentence must have a verb in it to be complete. **If it has no verb, it is not a proper sentence!**

We see and take part in thousands of actions every day. We **walk, run, speak, eat, sleep, learn, enjoy, annoy, love, hate,** and do a thousand other actions as well!

Examples:

> **1.** Every day I **walk** to school and **run** home.
>
> **2.** I **get** home, **do** my homework and then **play**.

Write down the **verbs** or action words in these sentences.

1. The train arrived at the station and left soon after.

   _____   _____

2. Hari drew while Jasmine painted a picture.

   _____   _____

3. The car turned left and stopped outside the library.

   _____   _____

4. The carpenter sawed the wood and then planed it down.

   _____   _____

Once you have learned your verbs, award yourself a star in the box.

Actions happen at three different times.

You write about an action happening **now**:
I **write**, we **race**, they **swim**, you **look**.

You write about an action that happened **in the past**:
I **wrote**, we **raced**, they **swam**, you **looked**.

You write about actions that will happen **in the future**:
I **will write**, we **will race**, they **will swim**, you **will look**.

> When writing about what **is happening now**,
> we use the **present tense**.
>
> When writing about what **happened**,
> we use the **past tense**.
>
> When we write about what **is to come**,
> we use the **future tense**.

35 After each sentence, say which tense the verb
is in – **present**, **past** or **future**.

1. I am. _____

2. They were. _____

3. The light shone in our eyes. _____

4. I will go to the ends of the earth. _____

5. After the rain the ground will be

   slippery. _____

6. They swim in the lake. _____

36 Change these from the present to the future:

1. I run. I _____

2. You like.   You _____

3. They listen.   They _____

   Change these from past to the present:

4. They painted. They _____

5. You spoke.   You _____

6. We drove.   We _____

Once you have correctly completed this
page, award yourself a star in the box.

167

Auxiliary is not a word we use very often but it means "helping."

What does it help? It helps a verb go into different tenses, or times. We use these words very often, although we may not realize we are doing so. These are some of the words used as helping verbs:

am	is	will	were	have	been	are	had

might	may	could	should	was

Here are some examples of how they help:

> I **am** walking. (**present**)
> He **will** sing too loudly! (**future**)
> We **had** finished the whole cake! (**past**)

The words **walking**, **sing** and **finished** are the main verbs and the words **am**, **will** and **had** are all helping verbs.

37 Write down **a.** the main verb and **b.** the auxiliary verb or verbs.
Example: She was drawing.
a. drawing. **b.** was.

1. I will come.

a. _____ b. _____

2. We were watching.

a. _____ b. _____

3. I am driving my car.

a. _____ b. _____

4. They had listened.

a. _____ b. _____

5. The children are playing in the park.

a. _____ b. _____

38 Pick out the auxiliary or helping words in these sentences.

1. They were feasting at the castle.

_____

2. When they had finished their meal, they could hear a knocking sound.

_____ _____

3. They were looking high and low.

_____

4. They might have heard a mouse.

_____ _____

5. They should have looked in the basement.

_____ _____

168

Once you have got 100 per cent, award yourself a star in the box.

The structure of a sentence.

So far we have learned that a sentence is a complete thought, and that every sentence has a verb, or word that expresses the action.

The first thing to do when looking at a sentence is to find the **verb** or action **word**.

> *Example*: **The monkey threw coconuts at the tourists.**

The **verb** in the sentence is **threw**.
The next question we ask is who or what threw?
The answer is the monkey
The **monkey** is the **subject** of the sentence.

To find the subject and verb of a sentence, ask:
1. What is the action? 2. Who or what did the action?

Here are a few sentences. Write down the **verb** and the **subject** of the following:

1. A large old house stood on a hill.

   Verb: _____   Subject: _____

2. No one lived there.

   Verb: _____   Subject: _____

3. The ghost haunted the old house.

   Verb: _____   Subject: _____

4. He rattled his chains.

   Verb: _____   Subject: _____

5. Nobody paid any attention to him.

   Verb: _____   Subject: _____

Once you know your subject and verb,
award yourself a star in the box.

169

TAKE A

This is the Pirates' map of Treasure Island.

Write down the clues in the numbered spaces provided.
Then read it!

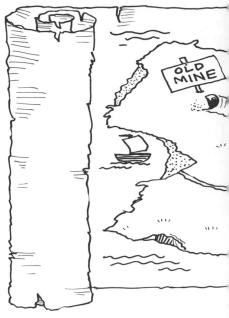

CLUES:

1. The **verb** in: **I will find the gold**.
2. The **subject** of this sentence: **Under the ground the treasure lies.**
3. The **verb** in: **Go quickly!**
4. The only word with "**i**" in it: **He looked into the water.**
5. The word that **describes** the castle: **The old castle was on the hill.**
6. The **subject** in: **The mine lay on the beach!**
7. The **verb** in: **We follow the long road.**
8. The first **noun** in: **Make a tunnel under the mountain.**
9. The missing **word** in: **What goes up must come _____.**
10. The missing **word** in: **_____ have I left my glasses?**

1. _____ 2. _____ 3. _____

4. _____ 5. _____ 6. _____

7. _____ 8. _____ 9. _____

10. _____

BREAK

Follow the clues and you will have the directions to find the buried treasure.

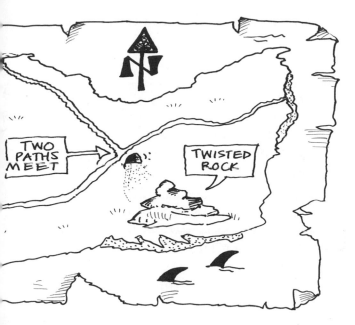

11. The **number** in: **There are two paths.**
12. The first **noun** in: **Walk along the paths across the fields.**
13. The **verb** in: **We meet again.**
14. The **verb** in: **At the crossroads turn left.**
15. **Not north, not east, not west but** _____
16. The **verb** in: **The gardeners dig the earth.**
17. The **word** that **describes** how he walked in:
    He walked carefully over the stony field.
18. The missing **word** in: **Not over but** _____ **the hill.**
19. The **word** describing the rope in: **The twisted rope stopped the lift working.**
20. The **subject** in: **The rock is heavy.**

11. _____   12. _____   13. _____

14. _____   15. _____   16. _____

17. _____   18. _____   19. _____

20. _____

Finding the object of a sentence

So far we have found the **verb** in the sentence by asking **"What is the action?"** and the **subject** by asking **"Who or what did the action?"**

All sentences have a verb and a subject and many sentences have an object.

The **object** is what is directly affected by the action.

Example: **The ghost haunted the old house.**

The **verb** is **haunted**. The **subject** is **ghost**.
The **object** is the **house**: it answers the question **"What was the action done to?"**

Here is another example: **He rattled his chains.**

The **verb**: **rattled**. The **subject**: **He**. The **object**: **chains**.

Write down the **Subject**, **Verb** and **Object** of the sentences:

1. André kicked the ball.

   Verb: _____

   Subject: _____

   Object: _____

2. The ball hit the window.

   Verb: _____

   Subject: _____

   Object: _____

3. Mrs. Park opened the door.

   Verb: _____

   Subject: _____

   Object: _____

4. "You broke the glass."

   Verb: _____

   Subject: _____

   Object: _____

5. "Not me! My ball smashed it."

   Verb: _____

   Subject: _____

   Object: _____

6. Mrs. Pank shook her head at André.

   Verb: _____

   Subject: _____

   Object: _____

Once you have correctly completed this page, award yourself a star in the box.

The **subject** and the **verb** of a sentence should agree, or match. This sounds complicated, but look at the example:

> The flower **is** growing.
> The flowers **are** growing.

The **subject** "flower" is **singular** or talking about **one flower**, and the **verb** "is growing" is also **singular**. The **subject** "flowers" is **plural** or talking about **many**, and so the **verb** must also be plural.

---

41 Choose the correct word to make the subject and the verb agree with each other:

1. The tree _____ (sway /sways) in the wind.

2. We _____ (was/were) going to Halifax.

3. They _____ (have/has) been eating.

4. The heron _____ (catch/catches) lots of fish.

---

42 Here is a short story. Choose the correct word from the brackets. Think carefully whether the verb should be singular or plural.

All the members of the family _____ (was/were)

reading quietly when there _____ (was/were)

a great explosion. Flames with lots of smoke _____

(was/were) pouring out of the kitchen.

"Someone _____ (has/have) left the oven on!"

exclaimed Dad.

"It _____ (was/were) me", said Mum. "I thought

I had turned it off but I must have left it on!"

"Everyone _____ (leave/leaves) now," shouted

Dad, "before the whole house explodes!"

Once you have made the subjects and verbs agree, award yourself a star in the box.

173

The number in the brackets tells where to look to remind yourself.

1. **Verbs**: (*Test 34*) Fill in the missing word:
   A **verb** expresses the _____ in the **sentence**.

2. (*Test 34*) Write down the **4 verbs** in these sentences in the spaces provided:
   The police car raced down the street, swerved around the truck, overtook the bus and screeched to a halt.

   a. _____   b. _____

   c. _____   d. _____

3. **Tenses**: (*Test 35*) Say which tense the verb is in – **present**, **past** or **future**:

   a. They will come _____

   b. The flowers blossomed in spring. _____

   c. The wind is blowing a gale today! _____

4. **Auxiliary verbs**: (*Test 37*) Write down the **main verb** and the **auxiliary verb** in these sentences:
   a. They were watching the game.

   Main _____   Auxiliary _____

   b. The ice cream had dripped on the carpet.

   Main _____   Auxiliary _____

5. **Subject and verb**: (*Test 39*) Find the **verb** and the **subject** of these sentences:
   a. The stars twinkled brightly.

   Verb _____   Subject _____

   b. Through the forest he galloped.

   Verb _____   Subject _____

6. **Finding the object**: (*Test 40*) Find the **verb**, the **subject** and the **object** of these sentences:
   a. The magician turned the boy into a frog.

   Verb _____   Subject _____   Object _____

   a. The frog ate the fly.

   Verb _____   Subject _____   Object _____

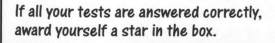

If all your tests are answered correctly, award yourself a star in the box.

PRONOUNS

Pronouns are really the **names** that we call **ourselves**.

I talk about myself as **I**.
I talk to my friend and call him **you**.
When I talk about him, I say **he** or **him**.
If I talk about a girl or a woman, I say **she** or **her**.
If I talk about a table, I say **it**.

These names are pronouns.

List A

I	he	she	it	you	we	us
they	me	him	her	them	one	

Examples:

I feel happy.	**We** know where **you** are.
She looked in every corner.	**I** gave **it** to **him**.

Here are some more:

List B

myself	yourself	himself	itself	themselves
oneself	mine	yours	ours	his	hers	theirs
someone	anyone	anybody	none	yourselves
somebody	each	all	some	herself	ourselves

As you see, these are names used by all people when speaking about things or people or themselves.
We often use a pronoun to replace a noun, like this:

Mark and Janine went down the road. **Mark and Janine** turned up the hill. **Mark and Janine** walked to the bus station.

becomes:

Mark and Janine went down the road. **They** turned up the hill and walked to the bus station.

Here we have used the **pronoun** to stand for the **proper nouns**.

Once you have learned your pronouns, award yourself a star in the box.

175

44 Find the pronouns in the following sentences.

1. They came to see us.

   _____   _____

2. We gave them a book.

   _____   _____

3. She saw the child in danger and called to him.

   _____   _____

4. When the computer failed to work, he hit it hard.

   _____   _____

5. You called the firemen and they came to put out the fire.

   _____   _____

45 From the **List B** on the previous page find the right words to fill these gaps:

1. _____ called a few minutes ago.

2. This is my book; it is mine. This is your book: it is _____

   This one is their book: it is _____

3. Has _____ seen my keys?

4. _____ of you should bring a lunch tomorrow.

Once you have found the right pronouns, award yourself a star in the box.

Mrs. Singh went into a shop to buy a sweater for her son.

> *"I want to buy a sweater,"* said Mrs. Singh to the assistant.
> *"What sort of material?"*
> *"Woollen,"* she replied.
> *"Any particular wool?"*
> *"Lambswool."*
> *"Long or short sleeved?"*
> *" Long-sleeved."*
> *"V-necked or crew?"*
> *"V-necked."*
> *"What colour?" "Blue."*

The word **sweater** is a **noun**. The words **woollen, lambswool, long-sleeved, V-necked, blue,** are all words that describe the noun **sweater**.

A word that describes a noun is called an adjective.

Adjectives usually stand in front of the nouns they describe:
The blue sea.
There can also be more than one adjective describing a noun:
A high, snow-capped mountain.

They can also stand like this:
The mountain was high and snow-capped.

Sometimes, the adjective might follow the noun:
The mountain, high and snow-capped.

From these sentences, find the **noun** and the **adjective** that describes it:

1. The crafty burglar crept into the old house.

Noun: _____

Adjective: _____

Noun: _____

Adjective: _____

2. He opened the oak door.

Noun: _____

Adjective: _____

3. He took as many valuable things as he could fit into his black sack.

Noun: _____

Adjective: _____

Noun: _____

Adjective: _____

4. Suddenly he saw the safe. The safe was strong and secure.

Noun: _____

Adjective: _____

Adjective: _____

Once you understand your adjectives, award yourself a star in the box.

177

An **adjective** describes a noun.

An **adverb** describes a verb.

> The ice skater danced gracefully to the music.

The word **gracefully** tells how or in what manner she danced.
Gracefully is an ADVERB.

Examples of **adverbs of manner**:

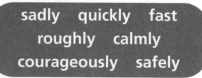

> sadly   quickly   fast
> roughly   calmly
> courageously   safely

47 Write down the **verb** and the **adverb** in the following sentences:

1. We left the concert hurriedly.

Verb: _____

Adverb: _____

2. The burglar crept into the house noiselessly.

Verb: _____

Adverb: _____

3. She spoke clearly.

Verb: _____

Adverb: _____

Adverbs not only tell you **how** or in **what manner** an action has been done but **when** and **where** it has been done.

Examples:
Adverbs of time: *yesterday, today, before, after, late, early, often, seldom, always.*
I arrived **late** for my appointment.
We **often** go to the cottage.

Adverbs of place:
here, there, far, near, everywhere.
They rushed **here** and **there**.
They looked **everywhere**!

48 Write down the verb and the adverb and say what sort of adverb it is – **manner, time** or **place**:

1. I will come soon.

Verb: _____

Adverb: _____

Adverb of: _____

2. They went there on Thursday.

Verb: _____

Adverb: _____

Adverb of: _____

3. In the earthquake zone, all houses must be built safely.

Verb: _____

Adverb: _____

Adverb of: _____

178

> Once you have understood your adverbs, award yourself a star in the box.

A **preposition** shows the **relationship between one word and another**.

The most obvious use shows the relationship between a verb and a noun. *Take this example:*

> I walked **up** the hill.
> I walked **down** the hill.
> I walked **around** the hill.
> I walked **over** the hill.
> I walked **beside** the hill.

In these sentences, the words **up**, **down**, **around**, **over** and **beside** show the relationship between the verb **walked** and the noun **hill**.

Here is a list of prepositions:

> about, above, across, after, against, along, among, around, at, before, behind, below, beneath, beside, between, beyond, by, despite, down, during, for, from, in, inside, into, like, near, of, off, through, till, towards, under, until, up, with, without

Notice how the **prepositions** are used in this sentence:

> The boat was moored to the post by the side of the river beyond the bridge.

to, by, of, beyond are prepositions.

49 Pick out the prepositions in these sentences:

1. We walked across the bridge and down the path beside the stream.

   _____
   _____
   _____

2. Look behind you!

   _____

3. The ship sank below the waves.

   _____

4. She stood beside the still waters of the lake.

   _____
   _____

50 From the list below, choose a suitable preposition to fill each gap:

1. The Channel Tunnel goes _____ the sea.

2. The sun dipped _____ the mountain.

3. We work _____ the bell goes.

4. She shouted _____ help.

Once you have successfully completed the test, award yourself a star in the box.

179

So far we have looked at the simple sentence. A **conjunction** enables us to join parts together to expand the sentence and make it flow better and sound more interesting.

Conjunctions join words, parts of sentences and sentences together.

Here are some examples:

> The vase was filled with roses **and** carnations.
>
> The sound of cracking glass **and** the sight of smoke made James run for help.
>
> We came **but** we found nothing.

In the first sentence **and** joins *roses* **and** *carnations*. In the second sentence **and** joins *the sound of cracking glass* **and** *the sight of smoke*. In the third sentence **but** joins the two sentences: *we came* **but** *we found nothing*.

Here is a list of conjunctions:

> and, but, or, nor, neither, because, since, as, that, if, unless, though, than, when, while, before, till, until, after, for, either, although, so.

51 Write down the conjunctions in these sentences:

1. The rain fell and the wind blew but the house did not fall.

   _____   _____

2. I could not go out because it was raining and I had no coat.

   _____   _____

3. Although he sent out SOS messages, no other ship came to help until it was too late.

   _____   _____

52 Which of the conjunctions listed opposite fit in the gaps?

1. The house has stood _____ 1600.

2. _____ we went shopping, the others made a fire.

3. _____ you do your homework now or you will have to miss the big game.

4. _____ the mountaineers were well trained, they still found the climb up the steep cliff very difficult.

Once you have completed this page correctly, award yourself a star in the box.

ARTICLES

These are just about the most common words and we use them in almost every sentence.

the   a   an

the is called the definite article.
a and **an** are the indefinite article.

Example:

> a beautiful flower grew by the garden wall.

a is the **indefinite article**.
It does not point to a specific flower.
the is the **definite article** because it points to a particular wall.

a *or* an

Whether you use **a** or **an** depends on the following sound. If the beginning sound of the word following is a vowel, then use **an**. If it is a consonant sound, then use **a**.

Examples:

a cup	**a** flower	**a** house
an apple	**an** egg	**an** orange

When a word begins with an **h** use **a** unless the **h** is silent, as in **h**our.

I will come back in **an** hour.

Words like "useful" begin with a vowel but have a consonant sound.

a useful gift.

Once you have understood your articles, award yourself a star in the box.

181

TEST 53

TEST 54

Write down **a** or **an** in front of these words:

1. _____ carpet

2. _____ high wall

3. _____ hotel

4. _____ hour

5. _____ school

6. _____ old man

7. _____ avenue

8. _____ useful tool

9. _____ autumn wind

10. _____ hedge

In this story, count how many times **the**, **a** and **an** are used.

Goliath was an ugly giant. He challenged any man in the enemy army to a fight. No one came forward because they feared the huge man. At last a boy walked towards him.

"I am David," he said. Goliath laughed loudly.

*A stream flowed between them. David chose some smooth stones and put them in his pocket.
He placed an oval stone in his sling, and whirled it round his head. He released the stone, and it struck the forehead of the giant. The giant fell over dead.*

There are _____ **the** s

There are _____ **a** s

There are _____ **an** s

Once you have found the correct articles, award yourself a star in the box.

A. Pick out the pronouns in these sentences.

1. They followed him to the house.

   _____ _____

2. That one is yours and that one is hers but this one is mine.

   _____ _____ _____

B. Pick out the adjectives in these sentences.

1. He carefully drew out the long, shining dagger. _____ _____

2. She watched the tall, graceful dancer perform the slow dance.

   _____ _____ _____

C. Pick out the adverbs of manner from these sentences.

1. The boy courageously took on the huge giant and skilfully killed him with a single stone.

   _____ _____

2. He ran back joyfully to his friends.

   _____

D. Pick out the adverbs of time and place.

1. I will go there today.

   _____ _____

2. We often travel far.

   _____ _____

E. Pick out the prepositions from these sentences.

We stood by the river looking at the new Millennium Wheel. We then waited in line for ages. Finally we went into one of the capsules. The view from the wheel was magnificent and we looked out over the whole of London. We could see over the rooftops and beyond the farthest bridges.

1. _____ 2. _____ 3. _____

4. _____ 5. _____ 6. _____

7. _____ 8. _____ 9. _____

10. _____ 11. _____

F. Pick out the conjunctions from these sentences.

Go beyond Greenwich and you will come to the Thames Barrier. This is a series of huge gates but they are not closed very often. They are closed if it rains to prevent the water causing floods. Unless the gates are closed the waters will rise until they cause damage through the streets of London.

1. _____ 2. _____ 3. _____

4. _____ 5. _____

If all your answers are correct, award yourself a star in the box.

183

You have covered **eight** parts of speech as well as looking at the structure of the sentence, that is, finding the subject, verb and object. **Well done!**

Now look at these sentences and fill in the gaps as instructed.

A A great river flowed gently through the sprawling city and out to the shining sea.

1. Three nouns: 1. _____ 2. _____ 3. _____
2. Three adjectives: 1. _____ 2. _____ 3. _____
3. One verb: 1. _____
4. One adverb: 1. _____
5. Two prepositions: 1. _____ 2. _____
6. One conjunction: 1. _____
7. One definite article: 1. _____
8. One indefinite article: 1. _____
9. The subject of the sentence: 1. _____

B Alfred completely defeated the ferocious Vikings at the battle of Edington.

1. Three proper nouns:
   1. _____ 2. _____ 3. _____
2. One common noun: 1. _____
3. One verb: 1. _____
4. One adverb: 1. _____
5. One adjective: 1. _____
6. Two prepositions: 1. _____ 2. _____
7. One definite article: 1. _____
8. The subject: 1. _____
9. The object: 1. _____

C Elizabeth, a just and brave queen, ruled the country wisely while her sailors defended the country from the mighty Armada of Spain.

1. Three proper nouns:
   1. _____ 2. _____ 3. _____
2. Three common nouns:
   1. _____ 2. _____ 3. _____
3. Three adjectives:
   1. _____ 2. _____ 3. _____
4. Two verbs: 1. _____ 2. _____
5. One adverb: 1. _____

Once you have got last test correct, award yourself a star in the box.

MORE SPELLING
TEST 57

As we said on page 129, if you are not sure how to spell a word or what its meaning is, you can look it up in a dictionary. In order to look up a word, you need to know your alphabet, as all the words in a dictionary are in alphabetical order.

Using your knowledge of the alphabet, start putting these cities of the world in correct alphabetical order. Remember, you will also need to consider **second** or **third** letters!

Oxford   Washington

London   Naples

Brisbane   Cambridge

Paris   Prague

Budapest   New York

Cairo   Nairobi

Nicosia   Bombay

Athens   Colombo

Berlin   Barcelona

Sydney   Moscow

Once you have sorted the cities alphabetically, award yourself a star in the box.

DICTIONARY WORK
TEST 58

Now let's see if you can put the world to rights!
These fifteen countries have got out of order,
alphabetically speaking!

Can you put them back in order?

Countries	Answers
Finland	1. Australia
Ghana	2. Cyprus
Greece	3.
Greenland	4.
England	5.
Cyprus	6.
Germany	7.
France	8.
Spain	9.
Grenada	10.
Gibraltar	11.
Uganda	12.
Portugal	13.
Russia	14.
Turkey	15.
Australia	16.
Gambia	17.
Sri Lanka	18.
India	19.
New Zealand	20.

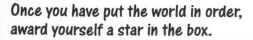

Once you have put the world in order,
award yourself a star in the box.

Magic "e" changes the sound and the meaning of a word.

bit becomes **bite**

and

hat becomes **hate**

Add magic "e", what do you get?
Read your answers to a member of your family.

kit	**kite**
sit	_____
fat	_____
at	_____
pal	_____
win	_____
twin	_____
spin	_____
can	_____
mad	_____
man	_____
pan	_____
van	_____
bad	_____
not	_____

Once you have completed this page, award yourself a star in the box.

 187

Listed below are some of the most commonly **misspelled words**. With practice you will become perfect. Get someone to test you. If there are any words that you don't know, look them up in a **dictionary**.

Wednesday	**sincerely**
rhythm	**doubt**
address	**although**
boisterous	**success**
February	**hymn**
surgeon	**grammar**
embarrass	**thumb**
either	**pigeon**
quarrel	**separate**
accommodation	
independence	

Once you have learned these spellings, award yourself a star in the box.

You know that two words may sound the same but have different spellings and very different meanings, for example:

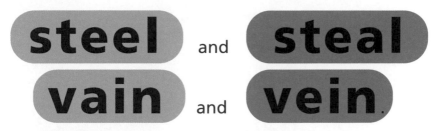

steel and **steal**

vain and **vein**.

Make sure you know the meanings of all the words.

Write out the sentences below, choosing the **correct spelling** from the two meanings so that the sentence makes sense.

1. There was a big *sail/sale* on at the shoe store.
2. Jack and Jill went up the hill to fetch a *pail/pale* of water.
3. *Our/hour* house is at the end of the street.
4. We use *flower/flour* to make bread.
5. There is a *hole/whole* in my bucket.
6. Music is food for the *sole/soul*.
7. The bus *fare/fair* was very expensive.
8. We want to *higher/hire* a gardener.
9. That *leek/leak* soup was very tasty.
10. The *air/heir* to the throne is Prince Charles.
11. Your *hare/hair* is very fine.
12. The clock struck *ate/eight*.
13. It sounds like the *whine/wine* of a wolf.
14. The *heal/heel* of her shoe needed a repair.

Once you have found the correct words, award yourself a star in the box.

189

MORE SOUNDS THE SAME
TEST 61

Now look at the words below, and for each word write in your notebook another word with the **same sound** but with a **different spelling**.

A star means you can write two answers!
Two stars means you can write three answers!

1. **mail**
2. **hale**
3. **led**
4. **bred**
5. **pane**
6. **reign**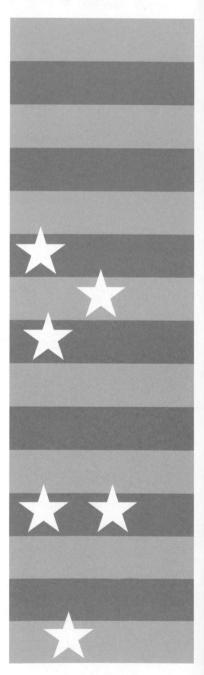
7. **so**
8. **two**
9. **knot**
10. **son**
11. **dun**
12. **write**
13. **there**
14. **here**
15. **buy**

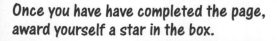

Once you have have completed the page, award yourself a star in the box.

IDENTICAL TWINS
TEST 62

Some words are **IDENTICAL TWINS** – well, almost.
They have the **same sound** and the **same spelling**,
but something is different. They have different
meanings.

Look at these two sentences, and you'll notice
ring in both, but with different meanings:

> a. It was a gold **ring**
> b. I'll **ring** the bell

Now find the **IDENTICAL TWINS** in these sentences:

1a. The duck's _____ was yellow.

b. The waiter handed me the _____.

2a. The terrorists were ordered to lay down
their _____.

b. A gorilla has long _____.

3a. Do you have the _____ to vote?

b. Good! Your answer is _____.

4a. The tree _____ was hollow inside.

b. Put your suitcase into the _____.

5a. Why do you always _____ him on
to be rude?

b. I'd like a hard-boiled _____, please.

Once you have found the correct twins,
award yourself a star in the box.

191

Now find even more **IDENTICAL TWINS**
in these sentences:

6a. My _____ sister is called Fiona.

b. She had a glass of _____ berry wine.

7a. I drew the square with my _____.

b. He was the _____ of the country for many years.

8a. There was a hole in the _____ of my shoe.

b. My grandmother enjoys Dover _____.

c. He was the _____ survivor.

9a. The ship sailed slowly into _____.

b. The old man enjoyed his glass of _____.

10a. She likes to wear tinted _____.

b. Beer is usually served in _____.

192

Once you have got 100 per cent,
award yourself a star in the box.

In English words **q** is always followed by a **u**, and we already know that the two letters together sound like **kw** when they come at the beginning of a word or in the middle of a word. A good example is **quick**.

Can you finish the qu words in this story?
Each dash stands for a missing letter.

The **qu _ _ _** promised to give a **qu _ _ _ _ _** of her kingdom to the first person to answer the twenty **qu _ _ _ _ _ _ _** in the royal **qu _ _** . James showed that he was **equ _ _** to the task by **qu _ _ _ _ _** giving twenty correct answers.

Dont forget another special combination is **ph**, which sounds like **f**. A good example is **photo**.

Can you finish the ph words in this story?
Again, each dash stands for a missing letter.

Suddenly the **ph _ _ _** rang. It was **Ph _ _ _ _** . He had spare tickets for "The **Ph _ _ _ _ _** of the Opera." I met him as soon as I had finished the **_ _ _ ph** for my Math homework. We enjoyed the show and were lucky enough to get a **ph _ _ _ _ _ ph** signed by one of the stars. Unfortunately, when I got home I had to start my **ph _ _ _ _ _** homework !

Once you have filled in the missing letters, award yourself a star in the box.

193

Remember how some English words can be difficult to spell because they contain **SILENT LETTERS**? A hundred years ago parents used to say that *children should be seen and not heard*. Silent letters are like this: **you must write them, but not say them**.

Don't forget that when a word begins with **kn**, the **k** is silent. When you say the word, it is as if it begins with **n**. A good example is **know**.

Can you finish the kn words in this story?
Each dash stands for a missing letter.

> Sir Galahad, the famous **kn _ _ _ _** gave a loud
>
> **kn _ _ _** at the oak door. Inside, an old woman
>
> was **kn _ _ _ _ _ _** bread, and another was
>
> **kn _ _ _ _ _ _** a shawl, while a third was
>
> **kn _ _ _ _ _ _** before the fire. Sir Galahad **kn _ _**
>
> they were the three witches.

Also remember that when a word begins with **wr**, the **w** is silent. When you say the word, it is as if it begins with **r**.
A good example is **write**.

Can you finish the wr words in this story?
Again, each dash stands for a missing letter.

> Jenny took her pen and **wr _ _ _** until her
>
> **wr _ _ _** began to ache. By this time her brow was
>
> **wr _ _ _ _ _ _** , and she knew it would be **wr _ _ _**
>
> to carry on. Jenny's younger brother was watching
>
> **wr _ _ _ _ _ _ _** on television, but she thought
>
> this was a stupid sport, and so she **wr _ _ _ _ _**
>
> a scarf around her neck and went out.

Once you have spotted the silent letters, award yourself a star in the box.

More words with SILENT LETTERS
In your notebook write the **correct spellings** for these 24 words:

1.	Go up	clim _
2.	Branch of a tree	bou _ _
3.	Information	_ nowledge
4.	Marks on paper	_ riting
5.	Contains a dead body	tom _
6.	Not a son	dau _ _ ter
7.	In your mouth	tong _ _
8.	Sailing vessel	ya _ _ t
9.	Four fingers and a	thum _
10.	Skiing holiday home	chale _
11.	Season	autum _
12.	Fidget	_ riggle

Try some more...

1.	Nice to eat	dou _ _ nut
2.	Part of a leg	_ nee
3.	How a rat eats	_ naws
4.	A number	t _ o
5.	For your hair	com _
6.	Garden ornament	_ nome
7.	Keep out of it!	de _ t
8.	Surrounded by water	i _ land
9.	Religious song	_ salm
10.	For cutting	_ nife
11.	Keep the dishes here	cu _ board
12.	Can prick your fingers	this _ le

	Once you have correctly completed the page, award yourself a star in the box.

195

How good are you at spotting spelling mistakes?

Improve your own spelling by finding and correcting the 25 mistakes in this story of Goldilocks.

One morning a littel girl called Goldilocks was walking through the forrest. Their were trees everywear, but suddenly Goldilocks saw a cottidge in an open space. Noboddy was at home. Goldilocks found boles of poridge on the brekfast tabel. One was two hot, one was to cold, and one was just write. She eight it all up. One chair was enoremus, one was tiney, and one broak when she sate on it.

Upstares one bed was harrd, one was soft, and one was so cumftable that Goldilocks fell asleep in it. When the three bares reterned from there walk, they were very angry with Goldilocks. She was so fritend, she ran back home!

Once you have spotted all the mistakes, award yourself a star in the box.

Remember the saying, "**i before e except after c**"? This is a good spelling rule to follow. It tells us that when **i** and **e** are next to each other in the same word **i** comes first and **e** comes second, as in the word **relief**. But it also tells us that when these two letters come right after **c** the order is changed, so that now **e** is first and **i** is second, as in the word **receive**.

Now let's see if you can apply the rule by finding the correct places for **i** and **e** in the following sentences.

---

1. The decorator is going to paint the **c _ _ ling**.

2. Would you like a **p _ _ ce** of cake?

3. Who is your best **fr _ _ nd**?

4. This is my nephew and this is my **n _ _ ce**.

5. There are five cows grazing in the **f _ _ ld**.

6. The doctor wants to see the next **pat _ _ nt**.

7. I **rec _ _ ved** some lovely flowers for my birthday.

8. The little kitten was very **misch _ _ vous**.

9. Do you **bel _ _ ve** in Santa Claus?

10. You should never lie or **dec _ _ ve** anyone.

Although this is a good rule, there are a few exceptions. The most important exception is **their**, where **e** always comes before **i**, as in the following sentence:

The children gave their books to their teacher.

		Once you have grasped this rule, award yourself a star in the box.	197

The story of Cinderella is as famous as that of Goldilocks. This version also has 25 spelling mistakes.

Use your magic wand to detect and correct them.

Cinderella's ugley sisters were horribal to her. They maid her do all the work: cleening, washing up, pollishing, laundrey and keeping the fiers burning. They wore beautifull clothes, while Cinders was dressed in rages.

One evvening the sisters went to a dance at the Prince's cassel. Poor Cinders was left at home. She begane to cry. Sudenly her fairy godmother apeared. "Don't cry," she said. "I will give you a wunderful coch, hansome horses, an elegent dress and prizeless glass slipers. Go to the dance, but leeve before midnight."

Cinderella danced with the Prince. She was so hapy she forgot the time. She rane home as it was strkeing midnight, leaving one slipper behind. This was how the Prince discovered who she was, and soon they were maried and lived happily ever after.

198

Once you have corrected Cinders' story, award yourself a star in the box.

TAKE A BREAK

In a dictionary there are thousands of words, but how many words can you find in the word **dictionary**?

Use the letters in the word DICTIONARY to build other words. You can put the letters in any order. Here are some suggestions to start you off:

act nation cat

We managed to find over a hundred words in all. If you can build 50 or more words from dictionary, you are doing really well!

1.	27.
2.	28.
3.	29.
4.	30.
5.	31.
6.	32.
7.	33.
8.	34.
9.	35.
10.	36.
11.	37.
12.	38.
13.	39.
14.	40.
15.	41.
16.	42.
17.	43.
18.	44.
19.	45.
20.	46.
21.	47.
22.	48.
23.	49.
24.	50.
25.	51.
26.	52.

TAKE A BREAK

This is the time to relax with a game all the family can join in.

In the word square below there is a mixture of vegetables: some you like and some you detest, and perhaps some you have not tried. Can you find 18? The words can be read across or down.

a	b	j	a	r	t	i	c	h	o	k	e
p	r	c	a	b	b	a	g	e	p	y	c
e	o	t	l	e	n	t	i	l	o	a	a
a	c	u	b	k	a	l	e	m	t	m	u
f	c	r	e	a	m	e	t	o	a	p	l
s	o	n	a	m	l	e	e	k	t	a	i
p	l	i	n	s	w	e	d	e	o	r	f
i	i	p	m	a	r	r	o	w	x	s	l
n	x	b	e	e	t	r	o	o	t	n	o
a	q	u	c	a	r	r	o	t	z	i	w
c	a	s	p	a	r	a	g	u	s	p	e
h	y	w	s	p	r	o	u	t	s	v	r

Remember that many English words have **DOUBLE LETTERS**, and a double instead of a single can make a big difference, for example:

> a **diner** is someone who is eating

> but a **dinner** is what the diner is eating **!**

Each of the words below has a **double letter missing**. See if you can write the full words in your notebook.

1. You blow one of these.   bu _ _ le
2. A jigsaw…   pu _ _ le
3. A French dog.   p _ _ dle
4. Try and solve the …   ri _ _ le
5. The opposite of nice.   ho _ _ ible
6. You do this with your eyes.   s _ _
7. You boil the water in this.   ke _ _ le
8. You blow one of these up!   ba _ _ _ _ n
9. You can kick this.   f _ _ tba _ _
10. Soldiers fight in a…   ba _ _ le
11. Beer is kept in this.   ba _ _ el
12. That … was really tasty.   pu _ _ ing
13. Another word for tummy.   be _ _ y
14. Opposite of sad.   ha _ _ y
15. The wet floor is …   sli _ _ ery
16. Cows eat this.   gra _ _
17. A vegetable.   l _ _ k
18. You put this up when the rain comes down.   umbre _ _ a
19. Something you do in your spare time.   ho _ _ y
20. This book is about …   spe _ _ ing

Once you have spotted all these doubles, award yourself a star in the box.

201

EVEN MORE
SEEING DOUBLE
TEST 72

We are still looking for double letters. See if you can guess these words without any clues.

A star means you can write two answers!

1. bu _ _ et

2. z _ _

3. p _ _ l

4. b _ _ t

5. w _ _ d

6. a _ _ ack

7. tr _ _

8. ki _ _ en

9. pe _ _ er

10. wi _ _ er

11. ba _ _ et

12. a _ _ le

13. ki _ _

14. su _ _ y

15. t _ _ th

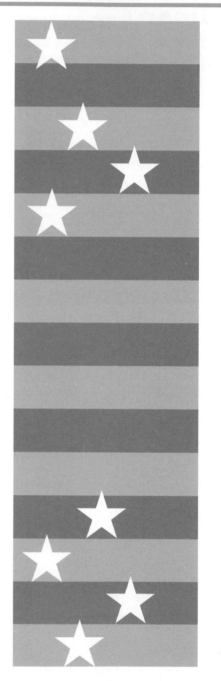

Once you have answered all these correctly, award yourself a star in the box.

ONE AND MANY
TEST 73

Remember how if we want to **change a SINGULAR into a PLURAL** we usually just add **s**? Don't forget, there are some other ways as well. If a word ends with a **y** we remove the **y** and add **ies** e.g. "poppy" becomes "poppies." Where a word ends with an **h** you often add **es**. Sometimes there are strange twists when we go from **one** to **many**, e.g. **mouse** to **mice**.

See if you can write the plurals for these words:

Be careful, there are a few difficult words to catch you out! To help you, there's an asterisk by the difficult words.

book	**fox**
house	**dish**
mouse*	**fish***
nose	**wish**
tooth*	**man***
poppy	**woman***
foot*	**potato**
child*	**goose***

	Once you have understood your plurals, award yourself a star in the box.	203

Try some more:

wife*	outlaw
girl	tomato
boy	axis*
motto	buffalo
piano	city
sheep*	leaf*
daughter-in-law	chief
memory	oasis*
roof	match
deer*	country
church	address
ox*	hoof*

Once you have mastered more plurals,
award yourself a star in the box.

– or VERSUS – er
TEST 75

Some names given to people end in **or**,
such as **doctor**, and others end in **er**,
such as **teacher**.

Can you work out which is the correct ending
to add to each of the following to make the person
complete?

1. **inspect** _ _
2. **organiz** _ _
3. **moth** _ _
4. **fath** _ _
5. **farm** _ _
6. **announc** _ _
7. **tut** _ _
8. **supervis** _ _
9. **murder** _ _
10. **hik** _ _
11. **angl** _ _
12. **runn** _ _
13. **act** _ _
14. **bricklay** _ _
15. **carpent** _ _

16. **lead** _ _
17. **direct** _ _
18. **produc** _ _
19. **dictat** _ _
20. **lectur** _ _
21. **speak** _ _
22. **creat** _ _
23. **minist** _ _
24. **mast** _ _
25. **learn** _ _
26. **box** _ _
27. **tink** _ _
28. **tail** _ _
29. **soldi** _ _
30. **sail** _ _

We know that action words (**verbs**) can have **ing** added to them: for example, **go** becomes **going**. But sometimes the addition of **ing** causes changes. Here are some guidelines to help you spell correctly when **ing** is added.

A. When the verb ends with e, take away the e before adding ing

e.g. **come** becomes **coming**

Have a go at these:

1. **hide** _____
2. **have** _____
3. **hope** _____
4. **drive** _____
5. **rinse** _____

B. When the verb ends with 2 or more consonant sounds (these are letters that are not vowels) simply add ing

e.g. **correct** becomes **correcting**

1. **swing** _____
2. **turn** _____
3. **collect** _____
4. **watch** _____
5. **stitch** _____

Once you have successfully completed this page, award yourself a star in the box.

C. When the verb ends with single consonant, double the consonant before adding ing

e.g. **clip** becomes **clipping**

1. **hop** _____
2. **stop** _____
3. **cut** _____
4. **put** _____
5. **spin** _____

D. When the verb ends with y, simply add ing

e.g. **simplify** becomes **simplifying**

1. **study** _____
2. **fly** _____
3. **carry** _____
4. **marry** _____
5. **fry** _____

E. There are some verbs that like to break these rules.

e.g. **be** becomes **being**

1. **tie** _____
2. **see** _____

Once you have correctly completed these tests, award yourself a star in the box.

Can you add the correct endings?
The sound at the end of the words is the same,
but sometimes the spelling is **al**, as in **comical**,
and sometimes it is **le**, as in **icicle**. Here we go:

1. natur _ _
2. partic _ _
3. deni _ _
4. refus _ _
5. dent _ _
6. rent _ _
7. whist _ _
8. department _ _
9. reliab _ _
10. admirab _ _
11. sing _ _
12. horrib _ _
13. ment _ _
14. met _ _
15. smugg _ _

16. edib _ _
17. fidd _ _
18. digit _ _
19. doub _ _
20. inflatab _ _
21. visib _ _
22. discip _ _
23. dispos _ _
24. divisib _ _
25. electric _ _
26. bicyc _ _
27. biodegradab _ _
28. dribb _ _
29. tri _ _
30. trip _ _

208

Most words, like people, live in **FAMILIES**.
The head of the family is usually a verb, such as **create**.
From this verb come the other members of the family,
such as **creator**, **creation**, **creature**, **creative**, **creatively**,
creativity.

Below are the heads of ten families. See if you can
write in your notebook three other members of each
family. Some possible answers are given at the back
of the book.

1. **act** _____ _____ _____

2. **move** _____ _____ _____

3. **think** _____ _____ _____

4. **produce** _____ _____ _____

5. **provide** _____ _____ _____

6. **direct** _____ _____ _____

7. **analyze** _____ _____ _____

8. **note** _____ _____ _____

9. **sense** _____ _____ _____

10. **enter** _____ _____ _____

When all your verb families are correct,
award yourself a star in the box.

209

Sometimes words are joined together in a sentence to make a **short form of sentence**. We often use this in speech when we want to be less formal.
For example: instead of saying ,
"My spelling is getting better." we can say
"My spelling's getting better."

The apostrophe **'** is very important, as it shows us not only where the words join, but that a **letter is missing**.

In the sentence above, the **'** shows us that the **i** of **is** is missing.

Occasionally **two or three letters are missing**, but one apostrophe is all that is needed.

In your notebook, write these sentences, using the short form.

1. I am working hard to improve my spelling.
2. My spelling is getting better.
3. Soon I will be very good at spelling.
4. You have been trying hard, too.
5. I can not learn all the words in the dictionary.
6. I must not forget to practise.
7. Pablo could not spell **contrariety**.
8. Although he had trained hard, he did not win the marathon.
9. Oh no, it has started raining again!
10. Lulu could not wait for the holidays to come.
11. My uncle said he would take me to Whistler.
12. I hope you are coming to my party.

210

Something added to the **beginning of a word** to make a new word is called a **PREFIX**.

Here are seven **PREFIXES** that change the meanings of words to their opposites:

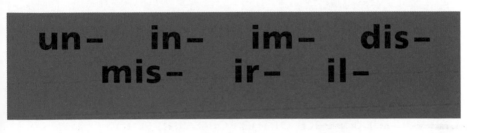

un–   in–   im–   dis–
mis–   ir–   il–

Can you choose the correct **PREFIX** to give each of the following words its **opposite meaning**?
A star means two answers!

1. possible	6. reliable
2. common	7. experienced
3. important	8. constant
4. place ★	9. obedient
5. respect	10. literate

Once you have completed the prefixes, award yourself a star in the box.

211

Something added to the **end of a word** is called
a **SUFFIX**.

Now here are seven **SUFFIXES**:

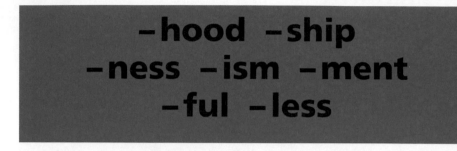

-hood -ship
-ness -ism -ment
-ful -less

Can you supply each of the following with
its correct **SUFFIX** ?
A star means two answers.

1. correct	6. leader ★
2. move	7. thick
3. child ★	8. member
4. childish	9. fellow ★
5. social	10. care ★

**Once you have completed this page,
award yourself a star in the box.**

If you are still not sure of the alphabet, now's the time to test yourself. First read it as set out below; and then try to say it without looking.

You really need to know the alphabet if you are going to be good at reading. This is because you might need to look up words in a dictionary if you do not understand them. You may also need to look up the names of places in the index to an atlas if you want to know where they are on a map. An index is also in alphabetical order; so, again, you need to know your alphabet perfectly.

Here are the names of some more of the world's cities. Can you put them all in alphabetical order?

PARIS
ROME
LONDON
JERUSALEM
DUBLIN
BOMBAY
CAIRO
MIAMI
OSLO
SANTIAGO
TORONTO
WINNIPEG
ATLANTA
ISTANBUL
AMSTERDAM

A
B
C
D
E
F
G
H
I
J
K
L
M

N
O
P
Q
R
S
T
U
V
W
X
Y
Z

Once you have successfully completed this page, award yourself a star in the box.

213

TEST 84

Can you find the odd one out in each of the following groups of five words, and say why the word is different?

a) SPANISH GERMANY DUTCH SWEDISH ARABIC	g) ROSE TULIP TREE DAFFODIL CROCUS
b) CHICKEN MONKEY COW SHEEP HORSE	h) PARIS CALGARY ASIA AMSTERDAM LONDON
c) DOCTOR DENTIST AUTHOR NURSE SURGEON	i) ROBIN OSTRICH SPARROW CROW CARDINAL
d) PLUM POTATO CARROT ONION CELERY	j) HERRING PLACE SALMON COD TUNA
e) GREEN RED YELLOW DARK BLUE	k) COFFEE TEA MILK JUICE BEER
f) DARTS BILLIARDS FOOTBALL TENNIS BASKETBALL	l) CAR PLANE BUS TRAIN TRAM

214

Once you have successfully completed these questions, award yourself a star in the box.

Choose a favourite book and practise reading a page of it aloud. Ask an adult in the family to listen to you as you read, and try to make what you are reading sound as interesting as possible. Stress the important words, and speak clearly. However, you do not need to shout. If anything mysterious happens in the story, lower your voice and slow down; and speak more loudly at a very exciting moment. If there are any very difficult words and you do not know how to pronounce them, ask an adult to help you.

Visit your local library often. They will have lots of books for you to borrow. During the school term, try to read at least one book every week. During the holidays, you might try to read two.

Sometimes it is a good idea to go to bed half an hour earlier than usual and use the time reading while you are tucked in warm and comfortably. But you must check that you have enough light, as you do not want to strain your eyes. You may even find a book is so enjoyable that you will not want to put it down.

Look after books properly, whether they are your own or from the library. You should not tear or scribble in them, and do not cut out pictures. If they are your own books, you can write your name in the front. The next time you have a vacation from school, try to write and also illustrate your own story. Choose from the following titles.

THE MAGIC CLOAK
ALIEN LANDINGS
A TRUE FRIEND
LOST AND FOUND
JOURNEY TO AN UNDISCOVERED ISLAND
NAUGHTY JONATHAN

Once you have successfully read this page, award yourself a star in the box.

215

Dinosaurs roamed Planet Earth for millions of years and became extinct 65 million years ago, long before human beings first evolved. Some dinosaurs were predatory carnivores such as T. rex, Allosaurus and Velociraptor. They would hunt smaller dinosaurs and kill them for food. Others, such as Diplodocus, Stegosaurus and Protoceratops, were more peaceful herbivores.

Paleontologists, scientists who study fossilized remains, have even found dinosaur eggs that are millions of years old. Some dinosaurs grew as tall as some of today's skyscrapers; but others, perhaps surprisingly, were small and only the size of chickens.

Did you enjoy reading the above paragraphs? Now try to answer the following questions.

1. Does a *carnivore* eat meat?

2. Find a word for a plant-eater beginning with H.

3. When did the dinosaurs die out?

4. Does a *predatory* creature a) sleep a lot b) hunt other animals for food c) have a hairy body?

5. Did dinosaurs lay eggs or give birth to live babies?

6. Were all dinosaurs huge beasts?

7. Name three meat-eaters mentioned.

8. Was Protoceratops a herbivore or a carnivore?

9. Has any human being ever seen a live dinosaur?

Once you have successfully completed this page, award yourself a star in the box.

Daniel's father always cooks certain meals on certain days of the week. If it is Monday, Daniel can be sure he will not make chicken or fish for supper. He never makes spaghetti or soup on Tuesdays. He does not like to cook eggs or fries on a Wednesday, and never makes salads on Thursdays. He will not make fries on Fridays, and never serves strawberries on that day either. He does not fry fish on Saturdays and on Sundays he always makes roast lamb.

On which day of the week might the family have the following meal?

Vegetable soup
Chicken, fries and salad
Strawberries and cream

Once you have successfully completed this page, award yourself a star in the box.

217

Read the short story below and then answer all the questions about it. You can look back at the story whenever you like and do not have to answer it entirely from memory.

It was cloudy and raining intermittently when Nick started to pack his suitcase for the journey from Charlottetown. Every now and then, the sun peeked out, but suddenly there would be a short shower. He was off to Vancouver the following day, Wednesday. Nick did not want to take too many clothes with him, so he decided to leave behind two of his six T- shirts and to take just two of his three pairs of jeans. The plane was scheduled to take off at noon, and the flight would take six hours. However, British Columbia time is four hours behind PEI, so he would arrive very early in the afternoon. It would be great to be on the west coast!

1. **On which day of the week did Nick start packing?**

2. **Was it raining non-stop as he packed?**

3. **How many T-shirts did Nick pack?**

4. **How many pairs of jeans did Nick leave behind?**

5. **Was Nick's plane due to leave at noon or midnight?**

6. **What time would it be in Charlottetown when Nick's plane got toVancouver?**

7. **What time would it be in Vancouver when he got there?**

218

Once you have correctly answered all the questions, award yourself a star in the box.

The following types of words all begin with capital letters wherever they are in a sentence:

- someone's name (first name and family name, such as Kelly Stevens)
- a city or country, such as Holland, Brazil or Madrid
- a language, such as Norwegian or Swahili
- a river, such as the St. Lawrence or the Fraser
- a title, such as Queen Elizabeth or Prince Charles
- the first word in any sentence
- the name of a manufacturer or store, such as Ford, Zellers or Harveys.

Practise writing out the alphabet with capital letters and then in small (lower case) letters as neatly as you can. Now look at the sentences below and write them out correctly, putting capital letters in the right places.

1. Sam travelled to spain and met his friend carlos there.

2. Ada has started learning russian and hopes to go to moscow next year.

3. we bought some food at iga.

4. Anna is italian and lives in milan.

5. Switzerland borders france, germany and italy.

6. Mr .and Mrs. cartier live in Ottawa.

7. Can you speak gujarati?

8. The seine is a river in france.

9. My favourite singer is avril Lavigne.

10. princess anne loves horseback riding.

Once all your capital letters are correct, award yourself a star in the box.

219

Here are some jumbled sentences. Can you put the words in the right order? Don't forget to put a capital letter at the start of each sentence and a period at the end when you write it out. Note that you will need to put a question mark at the end of three of the sentences.

1. favourite is sport lacrosse Mark's

2. are Saturday shopping we on going

3. birthday be my will it tomorrow

4. would like you holiday to for your go where

5. go you school today to did

6. Ottawa Canada capital of is the

7. her walk a takes four Fiona dogs every for day

8. on think do Mars you there are aliens

9. weekend going be fishing next will we

10. fries favourite is meal hamburgers and my

Remember that nouns are naming words. They name things, such as a BALL, a GATE, SCISSORS or an APPLE; and they also name people – CLAIRE, ROSIE, KEITH, for example – or places, such as AFRICA or GREENLAND. Here are some more examples: FEATHER, COMPUTER, HERRING, DUSTER, GARDEN, SNAIL, GEORGINA.

Now read the following short story and write in your notebook all the nouns that you can find in it.

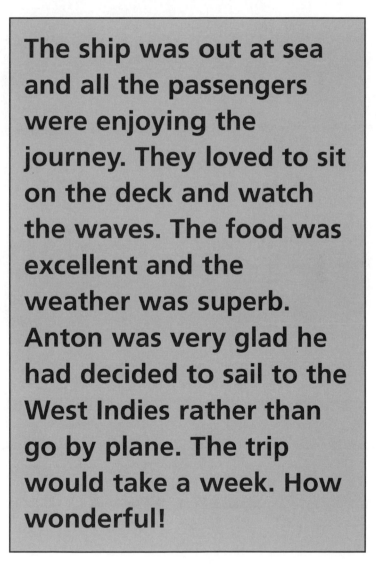

The ship was out at sea and all the passengers were enjoying the journey. They loved to sit on the deck and watch the waves. The food was excellent and the weather was superb. Anton was very glad he had decided to sail to the West Indies rather than go by plane. The trip would take a week. How wonderful!

Once you have successfully completed this page within 120 seconds, award yourself a star in the box.

221

Choose one word from those in brackets so that the two lines will rhyme because they end in the same sound. Then write down the two rhyming words in your notebook.

1. Jenny loved to romp and (*ride/play/spin*).
   She always did this every (*morning/day/night*).

2. Have you got a lot of (*money/toys/cheese*),
   To be enjoyed by girls and (*cats/friends/boys*)?

3. Pizza is so good to (*eat/have/gobble*);
   We always have it for a (*dinner/treat/meal*).

4. When you go on (*break/journey/holiday*),
   Send a postcard right (*soon/away/quickly*).

5. Do you have a dog or (*monkey/rabbit/cat*)?
   Is it thin or is it (*large/black/fat*)?

6. Because they like to eat (*ice cream/candy/
   burgers*),
   Have you one for all the (*boys/team/gang*)?

7. What is black and white and (*read/pink/blue*)?
   It must be a newspaper, I'd have (*said/thought*).

Remember that pronouns take the place of nouns and are always short words. WE, YOU, THEY, US, HE, SHE, IT, THIS, THEM, OURS, YOURS, THAT, HER, HIS are all pronouns.

Read the stories below. Then write them out in your notebook. But every time you come to a word/words with a star by it/them, change those words to a pronoun. See if you can get them all right.

Alice was upset. Alice* had misbehaved earlier in the day and Alice's* mother said Alice* could not have her allowance. Alice's* brother Bert, however, could have his allowance as he had behaved better. Alice spoke to Bert* about it and Bert* said that both could share his allowance. What a generous boy Bert* was!

Joy was just a little worried about going to her new school, but she knew that some of her friends were going there too. Joy* would be able to see friends* at break times. The girls* could all play together still, even if some of the girls* were in a different class. Joy had a new uniform. The uniform* was grey and red. It was nicer than Joy's* previous uniform.

Once you have successfully completed this page in beautiful handwriting award yourself a star.

223

Write out the paragraph below, putting in the correct punctuation – periods, commas, question marks, capital letters, exclamation points, quotation marks for speech, and apostrophes as necessary. Remember, each sentence has to begin with a capital letter, and a name has a capital letter. Periods go at the end of sentences. You need a question mark after a question has been asked, and an exclamation point if someone is saying how pleased or upset he or she is.

Julia's purse had been stolen i first noticed it was missing she told the policeman when i got on the bus and found that i didn't have my fare how much money was there in your purse the policeman asked i cant remember julia replied it probably wasn't much i spent most of it this morning buying john's birthday present how lucky that i had already bought it

TEST 94

Remember how an adjective is a word that describes a noun? STRONG, BIG, BRAVE, WIDE are all adjectives. They can be used like this: a *strong* boy, a *big* building, a *brave* soldier, a *wide* river. Look at the paragraph below, and as you read it, write down all the adjectives you can find.

> Andrea was impatient. She could not wait for her birthday party to begin. It was a very sunny day and so they were going to have a special picnic in the local park. Six of her best friends were coming and her mother was preparing a scrumptious lunch of sandwiches, jugs of cool, home-made lemonade and doughnuts. There was also going to be a marvellous cake and a fantastic magician to entertain everyone. What a wonderful treat!

TAKE A

You have been working hard at all the tests so far, so it's time now for some fun.

Can you put these eight pictures in order so that they tell a story?

BREAK

All the practice you have been getting in reading and understanding should help you with these.

Try to write in the answers to the clues for this crossword puzzle.

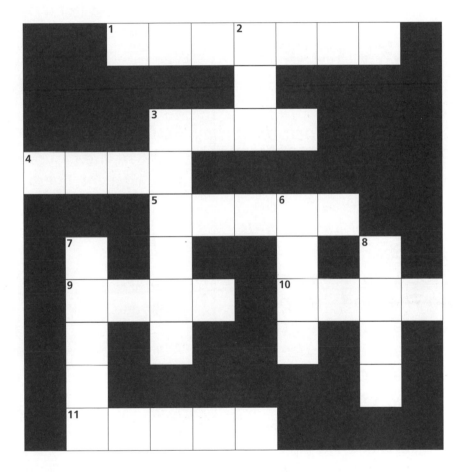

Across
1. Written on an envelope
3. Part of your ear
4. An elm is one
5. Seed of an oak tree
9. Vegetable
10. Small nails
11. To rest at night

Down
2. To steal
3. They grow on trees
6. Very thick string
7. A window is made from this
8. You can tie this with string

Read the following newspaper report and then answer the questions. You will probably need to look back at the report a few times to get the right answers. Note: there is one trick question!

Lucky escape

At least 1,124 people of 20 different nationalities, including families from Canada, were picked up by ferries after a fire on board the Sun Vista. It had been on a six-day cruise from Singapore to Thailand, stopping at the Malaysian city of Malacca on the way. According to one officer, who asked to remain anonymous, there were no fatalities due to good weather conditions.

1. What is the Sun Vista – a train, a ship, a bus or a plane?

2. How long was the cruise supposed to last?

3. Was anyone from Canada on board?

4. Did anyone die as the result of the fire?

5. Were there more or less than one thousand passengers on board?

6. Where did the cruise start?

7. Where was the cruise supposed to finish?

8. Where did it stop along the way?

9. What had the weather been like?

10. What was the name of the officer who spoke to the newspaper about what happened?

228

Once you have answered all the questons correctly, award yourself a star in the box.

Read each of the questions below very carefully before you try to answer it.

1. Is there a spelling mistak in this sentence?

2. Amy does not like jam or fish but adores cheese. Barbara hates eggs and tomatoes but likes ham. Carmen dislikes prawns but loves cheese and chicken. Jessica hates peanut butter but enjoys all sorts of fish.
   Which girl would like each of the following sandwiches?
   a) ham and lettuce
   b) cheese and tomato
   c) sardines and cucumber
   d) chicken salad

3. The day before yesterday, Francois was still 10. But next year he will be 13. How could that be true? It is!

Here are some headlines from the front pages of newspapers. Read them and then answer each of the questions on the right.

Corporal punishment might be banned in Sweden

Boy not yet 14 passes exams to enter university

John Major finds lost brother

Bank cuts 6,000 jobs

Constable wins lottery jackpot

Russia's prime minister fired

1. How many jobs have been cut by a bank – six hundred, six thousand or sixty thousand?

2. Is the person who won the lottery jackpot a painter, a policeman or a doctor?

3. Who found a long-lost close relative?

4. Will Sweden's parents be allowed to spank their children if the law goes through?

5. How old is the boy who passed his exams to enter university?

6. Which country's prime minister lost his job?

Once you have completed this page within 120 seconds, award yourself a star in the box.

TEST 98

Remember that a verb is a doing word. TO RUN, SHOUTING, WALKED, IS, WAS, WERE, SING, SANG, CRAWL, BUILD, for example, are all verbs. Read the paragraph below, and then write down all the verbs you can find in it. You should be able to write down 11 altogether.

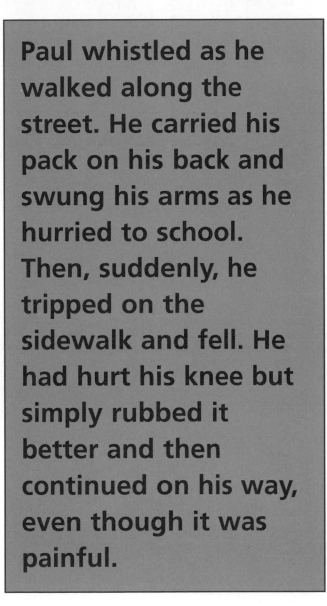

Paul whistled as he walked along the street. He carried his pack on his back and swung his arms as he hurried to school. Then, suddenly, he tripped on the sidewalk and fell. He had hurt his knee but simply rubbed it better and then continued on his way, even though it was painful.

Once you have successfully found all the verbs, award yourself a star in the box.

231

Read the following paragraph and then answer the question.

> John, Simon, Andrew, Lucy, Sarah and Milly all went to the circus. It was Simon's birthday and this was a special treat for his friends. However, there was a problem over who would sit where. Everyone wanted to sit next to his or her best friend. Milly wanted to sit next to Simon, and Andrew wanted to be next to Simon and Sarah. Lucy said she wanted to sit next to Sarah as well; and John also sat next to Lucy.

Can you make a plan to show the order in which they sat, if they were all in the same row. (There are 2 possible answers to this.)

Now read this paragraph and answer the questions.

> If you ever get a slight burn or a scald from hot water on your hand, the best thing to do is to run cold water over it for a few minutes. But if a burn is severe, you must go to the hospital at once.
>
> Long ago, people used to put butter on a slight burn, but we now know this does no good at all. If a blister forms, do not burst it. The blister protects new skin growing underneath and prevents infection.

1. Should you put a slight burn under warm or cold water?
2. Is it a good idea to put butter on the burn?
3. If a blister forms, should you burst it?
4. Where should you go if the burn looks bad?
5. What does a blister prevent?

Once you have successfully completed this page, award yourself a star in the box.

Remember that an adverb is a word that tells you *how* someone does something, and always goes with a verb and not a noun. Adverbs usually end in LY. SLOWLY, LAZILY, NEATLY, PURPOSELY are all adverbs.

Read the paragraph below and write down all the adverbs you can find in it.

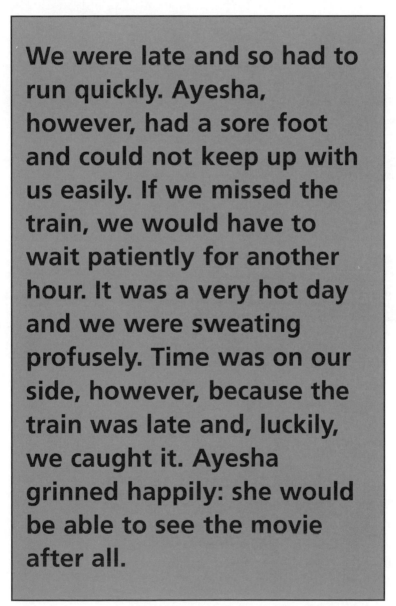

We were late and so had to run quickly. Ayesha, however, had a sore foot and could not keep up with us easily. If we missed the train, we would have to wait patiently for another hour. It was a very hot day and we were sweating profusely. Time was on our side, however, because the train was late and, luckily, we caught it. Ayesha grinned happily: she would be able to see the movie after all.

Once you have successfully found all the adverbs, award yourself a star in the box.

233

Read the paragraphs below and then answer the questions about them.

A healthy diet is important for growth. You need some fresh vegetables and fruit every day, since the body cannot store the Vitamin C they contain. There is a lot of Vitamin C in boiled potatoes, blueberries, broccoli and oranges.

It is best not to overcook vegetables so that they are soggy, as they will lose a lot of their goodness that way. Best of all are vegetables that can be eaten raw in salads: lettuce, bean sprouts, cucumber, tomatoes, carrots and celery are all delicious.

Do not eat too many sugary foods like cakes and cookies, and try to avoid too much candy and pop. Breakfast is the most important meal of the day because it gives you energy for school. Remember, too, that a crisp apple is a far better snack than chips or chocolate. You need some bread, and meat, fish, pasta, eggs or soy protein every day as well.

1. Should you cook vegetables for a very long time?

2. Is pop good for you?

3. Can celery be eaten raw?

4. What is the best kind of thing to eat between meals?

5. What is the most important meal of the day?

6. Where will you find Vitamin C?

7. Why do you need foods that contain Vitamin C every day?

8. If you do not eat meat or fish, what else could you have every day for protein?

234

Once you have successfully completed this page, award yourself a star in the box.

TEST 103

In the paragraph below, you will find some words with missing letters. Try to guess what each word might be and then write it down. The number of dashes shows the number of letters that each of the words contains.

As usual in a bung - - - - , Aldo's home had only one s - - - - -. There was a ch - - - - - because they often made a log fire on long winter evenings; and at the back of the house, Aldo's father had built a cons - - - - - - - - where his mother had an indoor garden. The family usually ate in the ki - - - - - ; but on special occasions, the table would be set in the d- - - - - room. Aldo's father kept his car in the ga - - - - at the side of the house. In case of intruders, they had a bu - - - - - alarm. In John's room, the colour sch - - - was blue and white.

Once you have successfully completed the missing words, award yourself a star.

235

Read the following story and then answer the questions about it.

Bobby and Tim decided to walk to see their grand-mother and give her a surprise. It was a fine day and their mother had said they could go. There would also be a chance to see their friends, Kevin and Brian, on the way.

Leaving at l0am, first they walked down as far as the post office, where they turned left onto Alexandra Avenue. Then they took the second right onto Ferncroft Road, where they stopped at the Baxters'. Fortunately, Brian and Kevin were in.

They only stayed a little while, and then continued down the road, taking the third left onto Manor Close where their grandmother lived. It was a cul-de-sac. Just as Mrs. Bolton answered the door, the boys heard her clock strike 11. She gave them a welcoming hug and asked if they could stay for lunch. There would be tuna casserole, and fruit for dessert.

1. **What were the names of the two Baxter boys?**

2. **What street do the Baxters live on?**

3. **What is a cul-de-sac: a road with trees, a road with a blocked end or a highway?**

4. **When the boys went to the see Baxters, did they have to turn left or right onto Ferncroft Road?**

5. **What is the name of Bobby and Tim's grandmother?**

6. **How long did it take them to walk to their grandmother's house if they spent just 15 minutes with their friends?**

7. **Did they turn right or left out of Alexandra Avenue on the way back?**

Once you have successfully completed this page, award yourself a star in the box.

Read the paragraph below, and then answer the questions. Try not to use a dictionary. You should be able to guess the meaning of any unfamiliar words from the story.

The elderly, amateur philatelist was a security guard by day; but each evening he would spend hours looking through his collection, even though it was just a hobby. His album was a fine one and there were some exquisite stamps in it from all over the world. He handled them gingerly. It would be a calamity if he lost or damaged any of them because he had spent so long building up this collection. It was always a delight to hear him talk so ebulliently about his wonderful collection.

1. What is a *philatelist*? Is it
a) a wizard,
b) a doctor,
c) a stamp collector?

2. What does *gingerly* mean? Is it
a) gratefully,
b) loudly,
c) carefully?

3. What does the word *amateur* mean? Is it
a) bald,
b) unqualified,
c) friendly?

4. What is a *calamity*? Is it
a) a surprise,
b) a blessing,
c) a disaster?

5. If you speak *ebulliently*, do you speak
a) fast,
b) in a whisper,
c) enthusiastically?

6. What does *exquisite* mean?
a) large,
b) beautiful,
c) unusual?

Once you have successfully completed this comprehension, award yourself a star.

Look for the word in brackets that is closest in meaning to the one *above*, and write down both words together.

You can use a dictionary for words that you do not know.

1. SHY
(YOUNG/ UNHAPPY/ AFRAID/ TIMID)

2. AVARICIOUS
(SPITEFUL/ GREEDY/ LONELY/ GUILTY)

3. PUTRID
(SOFT/ ROTTING/ WOBBLY/ NORMAL)

4. ESCALATE
(INCREASE/ DANCE/ FALL/ STARE)

5. BIZARRE
(SHOP/ ODD/ MERRY/ NOISY)

6. DONATION
(FRIENDSHIP/ COUNTRY/ ACTION/ GIFT)

7. ROTUND
(MOVING/ ROUND/ HAPPY/ BOLD)

8. FORLORN
(PRETTY/ GLAD/ RICH/ SAD)

9. IMPETUOUS
(TINY/ RASH/ CLEVER/ GENEROUS)

10. TEMPESTUOUS
(TEMPORARY/ NASTY/ ANGRY/ STORMY)

Once you have successfully completed this page, award yourself a star in the box.

ANSWERS

TEST 1
1. 70   2. 6   3. 5000   4. 800
5. -5, -4, -3 ... 3, 4, 5,

TEST 2
1. 25   2. 32   3. 42   4. 9   5. 9
6. 20

TEST 3
1. 431   2. 622   3. 364   4. 772
5. 617   6. 75   7. 255   8. $703

TEST 4
1. 2281   2. 4581   3. 6673   4. 2082
5. $3940   6. $4710

TEST 5
1. 2   2. 3   3. 1   4. 2   5. 0   6. 4
7. 4   8. 7   9. 3   10. 5

TEST 6
1. 22   2. 31   3. 42   4. 23   5. 41
6. 11   7. 21   8. 42   9. $57

TEST 7
1. 27   2. 49   3. 13   4. 27   5. 29
6. 3   7. 15   8. 17   9. $49   10. $45

TEST 8
1. 8   2. 9   3. 60   4. 18   5. 14
6. 12   7. 21   8. 18   9. 42   10. $20

TEST 9
1. 42   2. 52   3. 54   4. 57   5. 76
6. 95   7. $72

TEST 10
2. 666   3. 1305   4. 26199   5. 65968
6. 128232

TEST 11
1. 2   2. 1   3. 3   4. 4   5. 10
6. 9   7. 8   8. 12   9. 12   10. 6
11. 4   12. 8

TEST 12
1. 2r1   2. 3r2   3. 5r1   4. 6
5. 8r1   6. 8r3   7. 12r2   8. 4r1
9. 11r1   10. 7   11. 2   12. 4

TAKE A BREAK
The code message is:
NOW JUST RELAX.

TEST 13
1. 151   2. 163   3. 182   4. 193
5. 141   6. 141   7. 1203   8. 2513
9. 1365   10. 1421

Mrs. Johnson decides to pay $100.
She saves $104.75

TEST 14
1. 23   2. 23   3. 22   4. 23   5. 32
6. 31

TEST 15
1. 0.2, 20%   2. 0.1, 10%
2. 0.25, 25%

TEST 16
1. $\frac{2}{15}$ 2. $\frac{7}{9}$ 3. $\frac{9}{11}$ 4. $\frac{3}{7}$ 5. $\frac{6}{17}$
6. $\frac{3}{5}$ 7. $\frac{10}{17}$ 8. $\frac{2}{23}$

TEST 17
1. $\frac{4}{12} + \frac{3}{12} = \frac{7}{12}$

2. $\frac{5}{20} + \frac{4}{20} = \frac{9}{20}$

3. $\frac{2}{4} + \frac{1}{4} = \frac{3}{4}$

4. $\frac{3}{10} + \frac{4}{10} = \frac{7}{10}$

5. $\frac{4}{12} - \frac{3}{12} = \frac{1}{12}$

6. $\frac{5}{20} - \frac{4}{20} = \frac{1}{20}$

7. $\frac{8}{10} - \frac{1}{10} = \frac{7}{10}$

8. $\frac{7}{14} - \frac{2}{14} = \frac{5}{14}$

TEST 18
1. $\frac{12}{55}$ 2. $\frac{20}{63}$ 3. $\frac{2}{15}$ 4. $\frac{3}{14}$ 5. $\frac{1}{20}$
6. $\frac{1}{6}$ 7. $\frac{3}{50}$ 8. $\frac{2}{27}$ 9. $\frac{1}{66}$

TEST 19

1. $\frac{9}{14}$ 2. $\frac{1}{9} \times \frac{4}{1} = \frac{4}{9}$

3. $\frac{1}{5} \times \frac{2}{1} = \frac{2}{5}$

4. $\frac{1}{3} \times \frac{5}{2} = \frac{5}{6}$

5. $\frac{2}{7} \times \frac{2}{1} = \frac{4}{7}$

6. $\frac{1}{8} \times \frac{3}{2} = \frac{3}{16}$

7. $\frac{3}{11} \times \frac{3}{1} = \frac{9}{11}$

8. $\frac{2}{7} \times \frac{5}{3} = \frac{10}{21}$

TEST 20
1. 30°   2. 60°   3. 120°   4. 180°
5. 210°   6. 270°   7. 330°   8. 360°

TEST 21
1. 4cm   2. 5cm   3. 3cm   4. 3.5cm
5. 20cm   6. 24cm 7. 50cm
8. 500cm

TEST 22
1. 12cm²   2. 6cm²   3. 5cm²
4. 3cm²   5. 15cm²   6. 42cm²
7. 1.5cm²   8. 56cm²   9. 35cm²
10. 132cm²

TEST 23
1. 6cm²   2. 3cm²   3. 3cm²
4. 14cm²   5. 1cm²   6. 20cm²
7. 10cm²   8. 9cm²   9. 30cm²
10. 8cm²

TEST 24
1. 80°   2. 100°   3. 80°   4. 50°
5. 33°   6. 17°

TEST 25
1. 16   2. 25   3. 36   4. 49   5. 64
6. 81   7. 100   8. 121   9. 144
10. 1

TEST 26
1. 64   2. 125   3. 216   4. 729
5. 1000

TEST 27
31

TEST 28
89

TEST 29
a. 71 b. 63 c. 28

TEST 30
85

TEST 31
629

TEST 32
609

TEST 33
759

TEST 34
1. 5 2. 2 3. 4, 2 4. 7, 1, 2 5. 1, 5
6. 6312

TEST 35
649

TEST 36
905

TEST 37
a. 928 b. 331 c. 796

TEST 38
917

TEST 39
a. 5 b. 1 c. 4 d. 4
e. 1 f. 4 g. 6 h. 5

TEST 40
a. 4 b. 20 c. 11 d. 31
e. 11 f. 26 g. 11 h. 32

TEST 41
a. 15 b. 13 c. 28 d. 9
e. 55 f. 46 g. 45

TEST 42
a. 121 b. 476 c. 545
d. 488 e. 165 f. 227
g. 844

TEST 43
410

TEST 44
a. 131 b. 67 c. 154
d. 1581 e. 275 f. 55
g. 459 h. 158 i. 263

TEST 45
a. 110 b. 46 c. 78
d. 55

TEST 46
685

TAKE A BREAK
c
3 darts in ring 16 (48), 1 dart in ring
29 (29), 1 dart in ring 23 (23), = 100;
2 darts in ring 40 (80), 1 dart in ring
39 (39), = 119

TEST 47
1. a. 46 b. 106 c. 69
2. 22 miles

TEST 48
1034

TEST 49
343

TEST 50
a. 83 b. 401 c. 54

TEST 51
a. 1268 b. 1603 c. 9
d. 492 e. 172 f. 19
g. 48 h. 52 i. 83

TEST 52
707

TEST 53
a. $1,200 b. $106 c. 64

TEST 54
562

TEST 55
a. 130 b. 11.25am
c. 226

TEST 56
261

TEST 57
a. 195 b. 98 c. 460
d. 51 e. 154 f. 170
g. 504 h. 139 i. 136

TEST 58
a. 26 March
b. 21 June c. 21

TEST 59
378

TEST 60
1. 6am 2. 8am 3. 7am 4. 1

TEST 61
a. 1073 b. 1383 c. 49 d. 245
e. 239 f. 21 g. 579 h. 557 i. 284

TEST 62
898

TEST 63
a. 284 b. 53 c. 25

TEST 64
315

TEST 65
a. 1,115 b. 15,062
c. 222 d. 13

TEST 66
a. 160 b. 183 c. 296
d. 445 e. 308 f. 198
g. 99 h. 246 i. 37

TEST 67
a. 16 b. 12 c. 18 d. 14
e. 24 f. 6 g. 20 h. 22 i. 14 j. 12

TEST 68
a. 8 b. 6 c. 0 d. 2 e. 24 f. 3
g. 10 h. 11 i. 14 j. 6

TEST 69
a. 12 b. 21 c. 14 d. 36
e. 27 f. 24 g. 0 h. 3 i. 33
j. 15 k. 6

TEST 70
a. 48 b. 21 c. 48 d. 40
e. 28 f. 32 g. 12 h. 36
i. 8 j. 9 k. 20

TEST 71
a. 40 b. 80 c. 77 d. 55
e. 24 f. 18 g. 120 h. 110
i. 660 j. 10 k. 99

TEST 72
a. 35 b. 40 c. 24 d. 30
e. 28 f. 20 g. 15 h. 14
i. 45 j. 60 k. 55 l. 40

TEST 73
a. 60 b. 42 c. 40 d. 12
e. 54 f. 30 g. 0 h. 72
i. 24 j. 18 k. 12

TEST 74
a. 49 b. 14 c. 63 d. 28
e. 42 f. 56 g. 84 h. 7 i. 35
j. 21 k. 40

TEST 75
a. 24 b. 48 c. 15 d. 72
e. 32 f. 36 g. 56 h. 80
i. 40 j. 64 k. 88 l. 96

TEST 76
a. 18 b. 36 c. 63 d. 27
e. 72 f. 45 g. 81 h. 99
i. 54 j. 108 k. 0

TEST 77
a. 12 b. 120 c. 84 d. 88
e. 72 f. 48 g. 60 h. 44
i.96 j. 108 k. 144

TEST 78
1. $15 2. 54 3. 60 4. 60 5. $96

TEST 79
a. 24 b. 18 c. 0 d. 28 e. 108 f. 6
g. 50 h. 22 i. 14 j. 48 k. 2 l. 27

TEST 80
1. 48 2. $36 3. 12 4. 30
5. 36

TEST 81
a. 56 b. 108 c. 50 d. 44
e. 21 f. 48 g. 19 h. 0 i. 36 j. 20

TEST 82
1. 56 2. 14 3. 30 4. Yes
5. 144

TEST 83
a. 64 b. 81 c. 24 d. 30 e. 21
f. 54 g. 20 h. 15 i. 24 j. 33
k. 48 l. 36

TAKE A BREAK
21 pigs, 43 chickens
1. 0
2. 63 kilograms

TEST 84
a. 110 b. 1518 c. 539
d. 4556 e. 5372 f. 3304
g. 1980 h. 828 i. 1066
j. 1541

TEST 85
1. 20 2. $20 3. $12
4. 15

TEST 86
a. 8 r4 b. 9 r2 c. 11 r2
d .3 r1 e. 7 r1 f. 6 r2
g. 7 r6 h. 9 r6 i. 13 r1
j. 4 r1 k. 3 r1

TEST 87
a. 14 b. 13 c. 19 d. 16
e. 12 f. 20

TEST 88
a. 20 b. 22 c. 20 d. 45
e. 300 f. 21 g. 25 h. 106

TEST 89
1. 8 2. 45 3. 7 4. 27 5. 340

TEST 90
a. 5 b. 1 r73 c. 4 d. 3
e. 15 r1 f. 16 g. 109 h. 31

TEST 91
1. 60 2. 24 3. 24 4. 28

TEST 92
a. 136 b. 504 c. 567 d. 111
e. 940 f. 5274 g. 1805
h. 1659 i. 6601 j.19872
k. 0 l. 1360

TEST 93
1. 32 2. 17 3. 4392 4. 352

TEST 94
a. 0 b. 9,999,999 c. 10
d. 6 e. 12 f. 7 g 17 h. 40
i. 50 j. 420

TEST 1
1a. breathe, move from place to place, reproduce, grow, eat food
1b. none of these   1c. breathe, reproduce, make their own food, heal themselves when they get damaged, grow
2. **Living** – elephant, oak tree, human being, bee, cat, fish
Non-living – microwave oven, bicycle, bottle, train, stream, glass

TEST 2
1a.

1b. rabbit   1c. they would have no food
2. **omnivores** eat animals and plants; **carnivores** eat only animals.
3a. plant   3b. herbivore
3c. carnivore   3d. carnivore
3e. herbivore   3f. plant

TEST 3
1. To stay alive; to give energy; to help them grow; to stay healthy
2. They can make their own.
3a. fruit, vegetables, milk
3b. cola drink, chocolate, fries, beefburger, chips
3c. bread, eggs, baked beans, potatoes

TEST 4
1. 1 – g; 2 – b; 3 – h; 4 – a; 5 – e; 6 – c; 7 – d; 8 – f
2. fur, teeth, legs, lungs, claws
3. They fly.   4. They breathe air.
5. They keep warm, they fly, they breathe air and they eat food.

TEST 5
1. It pushes blood out of the heart and around the body.
2. 1 – b; 2 – c; 3 – d; 4 – a
3. Blood carries it around
4. **Good** – b, c and g
Bad – a, d, e and f

TEST 6
1. a. 105bpm; b. 70bpm; c. 94bpm
2. It gets faster   3. Your muscles
4. His heart beat

TEST 7
1. chest
2. To help us get energy from food.
3. In our blood
4a. resting;
4b. 2 minutes;
4c. it went up;
4d. it went down;
4e. 4 minutes

TEST 8
1. a – 1; b – 3; c – 4; d – 2; e – 5; f – 6
2. a – jaw; b – thighbone and pelvis; c – ribs
3. worm, slug and jellyfish
4. The skull and ribs are made of **bone** and form part of the **skeleton**. The **skull** is found in the head where it protects the **brain**. The **ribs** are found in the **chest**, where they protect the **heart** and **lungs**.

TEST 9
1. A joint connects bones together and allows you to move around.
2. **hinge joint** – elbow; **ball and socket joint** – hip
3. getting shorter
4. your arm moves up

TEST 10
1. a – incisors; b – molars; c – canines
2. A layer of bacteria
3. b – candy, g – cola drink; h – chocolate
4. To remove the plaque
5. 20

SCIENCE ANSWERS

TEST 11
1. a - sperm; b - egg
2. They have tails to help them swim
3. An egg and a sperm have joined together
4. Because most of them die
5. Producing babies

TEST 12
1. The amount of time a baby spends developing inside its mother's body before it is ready to be born.
2. a. an elephant – 22 months
3. c. uterus
4. From the mother's blood through the placenta
5. To provide the baby with all the nutrients it needs to grow, and to stay healthy herself

TEST 13
1. It provides them with food for growth and protects them from illness.
2. b-humans; c-elephants
3. So that they learn to talk and are able to communicate with others.
4. Feed them, clean them, keep them warm and protect them.

TEST 14
1. 1 – c; 2 – a; 3 – b
2. 12 to 15 years
3. 1 – b; 2 – c; 3 – a

TEST 15
1. a - 4; b - 2; c - 3; d - 1
2. a - 2; b - 3; c - 1; d - 4
3. Holds plant down in soil and absorbs water and minerals from the soil.
4. It links all the organs of the plant together; it holds up the leaves and flowers and it passes water and minerals to the parts of the plant that needs them.
5. b. to reproduce

TEST 16
1. The process by which plants make food
2. Water, carbon dioxide and light
3. There is more sunlight and it is warmer
4. The grass got no light
5. a - water; b - light; c - food

TEST 17
1. a – anther and filament; b – carpel; c – ovary; d – anther

TEST 18
1. The transfer of pollen from the male part of a flower to the female part of another flower
2. **Insect pollination** – the pollen is carried by insects, such as bees. **Wind pollination** – the pollen is carried by the wind.
3. Roses are insect pollinated; Grass is wind pollinated.
4. Pollen lands on the stigma.

TEST 19
1. Tiny baby plant and food store
2. Spreading out the seeds
3. Maple seeds are dispersed by the wind. Blackberries are dispersed by insects or birds (and other animals)
4. They would not get enough food or light and would die.

TEST 20
1. When a seed grows into a baby plant
2. Water, warmth and oxygen
3. It is too cold
4. a – to find water. b – to reach the light

TEST 21
1. b – a type of energy
2. **Batteries** – a, f and g. **Outlets** – b, c, d and e
3. Microwave oven, stove, kettle, washing machine, clothes dryer, dishwasher, iron, radio, food processor, toaster, etc.

TEST 22
1. **Heat conductors** – aluminum, copper wire, metal saucepan, iron, gold
Heat insulators – plastic cup, wooden stick, string, paper
Electrical conductors – metal saucepan, copper wire, silver bracelet
Electrical insulators – wooden stick, plastic cup, china plate
2a. It allows heat to pass through it
2b. It does not allow electricity to pass through it

TEST 23
1. a push or a pull
2a. gravity and upthrust
2b. the forces are balanced
2c. the boat would sink

TEST 24
1. b - a type of force
2. No, he can get the steel keys only. Copper is not attracted to magnets
3. iron, cobalt, nickel and steel
4a. they will repel
4b. they will attract

TEST 25
1. c - a type of energy
2. a, c, d and f
3. statement c
4. glass is transparent so light travels through it, but bricks are not and light cannot get through.

TEST 26
1. It is moving back and forth
2. By air particles vibrating
3. c - air; b - water; a - metal pipe
4. Because there is no air and therefore no particles to carry the sound.

TEST 27
1. **Solids** – wood, glass, ice
Liquids – orange juice, blood
Gases – oxygen, water vapour, carbon dioxide
2. It turns back into a liquid
3. 1 – b; 2 – c; 3 – a

TEST 28
1. **Wood** – hard and strong
Clingwrap – flexible and waterproof
Glass – brittle, hard and waterproof
Metal – hard, strong and waterproof
Cloth – flexible
2. 1 – c; 2 – e; 3 – b; 4 – d; 5 – a
3. c – liquids flow and solids do not

ENGLISH
TEST 1
ape, ball, cheese, dog, easy, frog, grass, heel, igloo, jam, kettle, loud, mat, nail, orange, piano, queen, read, skin, town, under, van, wedding, X-ray, yellow, zoo

TEST 2
salad, sandwich, scent, school, seat, sleep, sling, slot, snooze, soap, soldier, soup, special, sport, spot, station, stone, strap, sun, syrup

TEST 3
Steven Allsop, Jenny Andrews, James Brown, Michael Dixon, Luke Dougall, Andrew Dubois, Sarah Glass, Brian Gross, Keesha Johnson, Frank Kent, Amber Kim, Reem Mahdi, Robert Marks, Rosie Mitchell, Emily Parsons, Donna Patel, Karen Simons, Barnaby Smith, Anna Storr, Alice Thompson, Alison Turner, Paul Yee

TEST 4
HAND, SAND, SEND, LEND, BEND, BEAD, HEAD, HEAR, BEAR, NEAR

TEST 5
cold, bed, hot, better, slept
skates, proud, wear, time, goal

TEST 6
1. quest 2. quickly 3. quarter
4. quiet 5. quack 6. question

ENGLISH

ANSWERS

TEST 7
1. write 2. wring 3. wrong 4. wrist
5. wriggling 6. wreath

TEST 8
1. KNOT 2. KNEEL 3. KNUCKLES
4. KNIT 5. KNOCK
6. photographs
7. autograph
8. pharmacist
9. telephone

TEST 9
1. received 2. thief 3. believe
4. chief 5. grief 6. brief 7. relief
8. heir 9. Their 10. seized

TEST 10
1. sign 2. comb 3. wheels
4. limb 5. knee 6. whole
7. ghost 8. gnome 9. gnaw
10. wrench 11. COUGH
12. LAUGH 13. PITCH
14. RUSH

TEST 11
1. piece 2. pier 3. deer
4. tiers 5. doe 6. thyme
7. knows 8. need, steel
9. missed 10. grown
11. seen 12. heard
13. teem 14. caught

TEST 12
1. countries 2. potatoes
3. babies 4. libraries
5. classes 6. Scotsmen
7. ladies 8. sheep

TEST 13
CHERRY FIG MELON BANANA PLUM
MANGO PEAR APPLE ORANGE
PEACH
ENGLAND CANADA SCOTLAND
WALES POLAND RUSSIA BRAZIL
EGYPT SPAIN ITALY

TEST 14
weeding, Wednesday, would, whole,
there, rose, borders, medal, to,
flowers
to, friends, would, wear, new, were,
plain, red, hoped, great

TAKE A BREAK
EDIBLE, FASHIONABLE, HORRIBLE,
PORTABLE, WASHABLE, ILLEGIBLE

1. THOUGH – 10. SLOW
2. STRAW – 7. POOR
3. PLATE – 5. EIGHT
4. MIGHT – 11. KITE
6. LAUGH – 12. STAFF
8. VIEW – 9. SHOE

TEST 15
goldfish, perfectly, bored,
backwards, forwards, seemed, one,
two, weather, pair
Christmas, presents, knew, chimney,
too, turkey, potatoes, corn, be, sure

TEST 16
1. PHOTOGRAPHS
2. ANGRY
3. BUTTERFLY
4. GUITAR
5. FOOTBALL
6. SPAGHETTI
7. COLONEL
8. ORCHESTRA
9. DROUGHT
10. LEMONADE
11. EXTRAORDINARY
12. BRONZE
13. JUPITER

TEST 17
1. television 2. station
3. lotion 4. indigestion
5. fiction 6. information
7. destination 8. vision
9. mansion 10. potion
11. portion 12. pension
13. caution 14. motion

TEST 18
1. boar 2. raw 3. roar
4. oar 5. more 6. saw
7. draw 8. drawers 9. trawler
10. core 11. bore 12. soar
13. sore 14. terror
15. dawn

TEST 19
1. barrel 2. address
3. butter 4. messy 5. roof
6. occupied 7. luggage
8. communicate 9. beef
10. accident

TEST 20
1. Three, through, threw
2. sweet, swan, sword
3. where, whether, what
4. score, scenery
5. know, knot, knee, kneads
6. treasure, try, try, trips
7. sty, Steak, sting, stop, straight

TEST 21
1. complete 2. incomplete
3. incomplete 4. complete
5. incomplete 6. complete
7. incomplete

TEST 22
1. shone 2. gathered
3. fell 4. car 5. beach

TEST 23
1. e 2. a 3. f 4. g 5. b
6. c 7. d

TEST 24
1. statement
2. command
3. statement
4. statement
5. exclamation
6. statement
7. question

TEST 25
1. ! 2. ? 3. ! 4. ! 5. ? 6. !
7. ? 8. . 9. ! 10. .

TEST 26
1. sun, sea 2. birds, river
3. boat, rock 4. apple, pear
5. chocolates, ice cream

TEST 27
1. Alex, Sarah, Winnipeg
2. Smith, Jones, Montreal
3. Paris, Helen, Sparta, Menelaus,
Troy 4. Hannah, Tom, Windsor

TEST 28
1. flock, shoal 2. fleets, gang
3. forests, pack

TEST 29
1. singular 2. plural
3. plural 4. singular 5. plural

TEST 30
1. flowers 2. tables 3. pianos,
4. houses 5. potatoes
6. tomatoes 7. countries
8. replies 9. skies 10. buses
11. dishes 12. matches 13. halves
14. leaves 15. shelves 16. deer,
moose, salmon, squid, etc.

TEST 31
1. complete 2. incomplete
3. incomplete 4. complete

TEST 32
1. ! command 2. ? question
3. . statement 4. . *or* ! command

TEST 33
1. Menelaus, Sparta, Helen
2. cluster, string
3. king, woman, wife, diamonds,
neck

TEST 34
1. arrived, left 2. drew, painted
3. turned, stopped
4. sawed, planed

TEST 35
1. present 2. past 3. past
4. future 5. future 6. present

TEST 36
1. I will run 2. You will like
3. They will listen 4. They paint
5. You speak 6. We drive

TEST 37
1a. come 1b. will 2a. watching
2b. were 3a. driving 3b. am
4a. listened 4b. had 5a. playing
5b. are

TEST 38
1. were   2. had, could   3. were
4. might have   5. should have

TEST 39
1. stood, house   2. lived, no one
3. haunted, ghost   4. rattled, he
5. paid, nobody

TAKE A BREAK
1. find   2. treasure   3. go
4. into   5. old   6. mine
7. follow   8. tunnel   9. down
10. where   11. two   12. paths
13. meet   14. turn   15. south
16. dig   17. carefully   18. under
19. twisted   20. rock

TEST 40
1. kicked, Joseph, ball   2. hit, ball,
window   3. opened, Mrs Jones,
door   4. broke, you, glass
5. smashed, ball, it   6. shook, Mrs
Jones, broom

TEST 41
1. sways   2. were   3. have
4. catches

TEST 42
were, was, were, has, was, leave

TEST 43
1. action   2a. raced   2b. swerved
2c. overtook   2d. screeched
3a. future   3b. past   3b. present
4a. watching, were   4b. dripped,
had   5a. twinkled, stars
5b. galloped, he   6a. turned,
magician, boy   6b. ate, frog, fly

TEST 44
1. They, us   2. we, them
3. she, him   4. he, it   5. you, they

TEST 45
1. someone or somebody
2. yours, theirs
3. anyone or anybody   4. each,
none, all, some

TEST 46
1. burglar, crafty, house, old
2. door, oak
3. things, valuable, sack, black
4. safe, strong, secure

TEST 47
1. V. left, Adv. hurriedly
2. V. crept, Adv. noiselessly
3. V. spoke, Adv. clearly

TEST 48
1. will come, soon, time
2. went, there, place
3. must be built, safely, manner

TEST 49
1a. across   1b. down   1c. beside
2. behind   3. below   4. beside, of

TEST 50
1. under   2. behind   3. until
4. for

TEST 51
1. and, but   2. because, and
3. although, until

TEST 52
1. since   2. while, because, before,
after   3. either   4. although

TEST 53
1. a   2. a   3. a   4. an   5. a   6. an
7. an   8. a   9. an   10. a

TEST 54
6 x the, 3 x a, 2 x an

TEST 55
A1. They, him   A2. yours, hers,
mine   B1. long, shining
B2. tall, graceful, slow
C1. courageously, skilfully
C2. joyfully   D1. there, today
D2. often, far   E1. by   E2. at
E3. in   E4. for   E5. into   E6. of
E7. from   E8. at   E9. of   E10. over
E11. beyond   F1. and   F2. but
F3. if   F4. unless   F5. until

TEST 56
A1. river, city, sea   A2. great, sprawling, shining   A3. flowed
A4. gently   A5. through, to
A6. and   A7. the   A8. a   A9. river
B1. Alfred, Vikings, Edington
B2. battle   B3. defeated
B4. completely   B5. ferocious
B6. at, of   B7. the   B8. Alfred
B9. Vikings
C1. Elizabeth, Armada, Spain
C2. queen, country, sailors,
C3. just, brave, mighty
C4. ruled, defended
C5. wisely

TEST 57
Athens, Barcelona, Berlin, Bombay, Brisbane, Budapest, Cairo, Cambridge, Colombo, London, Moscow, Nairobi, Naples, New York, Nicosia, Oxford, Paris, Prague, Sydney, Washington

TEST 58
Australia, Cyprus, England, Finland, France, Gambia, Germany, Ghana, Gibraltar, Greece, Greenland, Grenada, India, New Zealand, Portugal, Russia, Spain, Sri Lanka, Turkey, Uganda

TEST 59
kit, kite   sit, site   fat, fate
at, ate   pal, pale   win, wine
twin, twine   spin, spine
can, cane   mad, made
man, mane   pan, pane
van, vane   bad, bade
not, note

TEST 60
1. sale   2. pail   3. our   4. flour
5. hole   6. soul   7. fare   8. hire
9. leek   10. heir   11. hair
12. eight   13. whine   14. heel

TEST 61
1. male   2. hail   3. lead   4. bread
5. pain   6. rain, rein   7. sow, sew
8. too, to   9. not   10. sun
11. done   12. right, rite, wright
13. their   14. hear   15. by, bye

TEST 62 & 63
1. bill   2. arms   3. right   4. trunk
5. egg
6. elder   7. ruler   8. sole
9. port   10. glasses

TEST 64
queen, quarter, questions, quiz, equal, quickly/quietly,
phone, Philip, Phantom, graph, photograph, physics

TEST 65
knight , knock, kneading, knitting, kneeling, knew,
wrote, wrist, wrinkled, wrong, wrestling, wrapped

TEST 66
1. climb   2. bough   3. knowledge
4. writing   5. tomb   6. daughter
7. tongue   8. yacht   9. thumb
10. chalet   11. autumn   12. wriggle

TEST 67
1. doughnut   2. knee
3. gnaws   4. two   5. comb
6. gnome   7. debt   8. island
9. psalm   10. knife   11. cupboard
12. thistle

TEST 68
little, forest, there, everywhere, cottage, nobody, bowls, porridge, breakfast, table, too, too, right, ate, enormous, tiny, broke, sat, upstairs, hard, comfortable, bears, returned, their, frightened

TEST 69
1. ceiling   2. piece   3. friend
4. niece   5. field   6. patient
7. received   8. mischievous
9. believe   10. deceive

TEST 70
ugly, horrible, made, cleaning, polishing, laundry, fires, beautiful, rags, evening, castle, began, suddenly, appeared, wonderful, coach, handsome, elegant, priceless, slippers, leave, happy, ran, striking, married

250

ENGLISH ANSWERS

TAKE A BREAK "DICTIONARY"
acid , acidity, acorn, acrid, act, action, actor, aid, air, airy, an, and, ant, any, arc, arid, art, arty, at, ay, cad, cairn, can, candy, cant, car, card, cart, carton, cat, city, coat, cod, con, corn, corny, coy, crayon, crony, cry, dainty, dairy, darn, dart, day, diary, diction, din, dint, dirt, dirty, don, dot, drain, dray, dry, icon, icy, in, into, ion, it, nard, nay, nit, no, nod, nor, not, notary, nation, racy, radii, radio, radon, raid, rain, rainy, ran, rancid, rant, rat, ration, ray, rayon, rid, rind, riot, roc, rod, rot, rota, tan, tar, tardy, tarn, tidy, tin, tiny, to, toad, tod, today, ton, tor, torn, toy, train, tray, triad, trio, try, yon

WORD SQUARE
artichoke, asparagus, bean, beet, broccoli, cabbage, carrot, cauliflower, kale, leek, lentil, parsnip, pea, potato, spinach, sprouts, turnip, yam

TEST 71
1. bubble   2. puzzle   3. poodle
4. riddle   5. horrible   6. see
7. kettle   8. balloon   9. football
10. battle   11. barrel   12. pudding
13. belly   14. happy   15. slippery
16. grass   17. leek   18. umbrella
19. hobby   20. spelling

TEST 72
1. bullet, buffet   2. zoo
3. peel, pool   4. beet, boot
5. weed, wood   6. attack   7. tree
8. kitten   9. pepper   10. winner
11. ballet   12. addle, apple
13. kill, kiss   14. sully, sunny
15. teeth, tooth

TEST 73
1. books   2. houses   3. mice
4. noses   5. teeth   6. poppies
7. feet   8. children   9. foxes
10. dishes   11. fish or fishes
12. wishes   13. men   14. women
15. potatoes   16. geese

TEST 74
17. wives   18. girls   19. boys
20. mottos or mottoes   21. pianos
22. sheep   23. daughters-in-law
24. memories   25. roofs   26. deer
27. churches   26. outlaws
29. tomatoes   30. axes
31. buffalo or buffaloes   32. cities
33. leaves   34. chiefs   35. oases
36. matches   37. countries
38. addresses 39. oxen 40. hooves

TEST 75
1. inspector   2. organizer
3. mother   4. father   5. farmer
6. announcer   7. tutor
8. supervisor   9. murderer
10. hiker   11. angler   12. runner
13. actor   14. bricklayer
15. carpenter   16. leader
17. director   18. producer
19. dictator   20. lecturer
21. speaker   22. creator
23. minister   24. master
25. learner   26. boxer   27. tinker
28. tailor   29. soldier   30. sailor

TEST 76
A1. hiding   A2. having
A3. hoping   A4. driving
A5. rinsing   B1. swinging
B2. turning   B3. collecting
B4. watching   B5. stitching

TEST 77
C1. hopping   C2. stopping
C3. cutting   C4. putting
C5. spinning   D1. studying
D2. flying   D3. carrying
D4. marrying   D5. frying
E1. tying   E2. seeing

TEST 78
1. natural   2. particle   3. denial
4. refusal   5. dental   6. rental
7. whistle   8. departmental
9. reliable   10. admirable
11. single   12. horrible   13. mental
14. metal   15. smuggle   16. edible
17. fiddle   18. digital   19. double
20. inflatable   21. visible
22. disciple   23. disposal
24. divisible   25. electrical
26. bicycle   27. biodegradable
28. dribble   29. trial   30. triple

251

TEST 79

1. actor, action, active, actively, activate, activity   2. movement, mover, moveable/movable,
3. thinker, thought, thoughtful, thinking, thoughtfully, thoughtless, thoughtlessly   4. production, producer, productive, productively,
5. provision, provider, providence, providential, provident, providentially
6. direction, director, directive, directional, directly, directory
7. analysis, analyst, analytical
8. notate, notation, notable, notelet, noteworthy, notary, notorious, notion
9. sensor, sensible, sensibility, sensation, sensational
10. entrant, entry, entrance

TEST 80

1. I'm working hard to improve my spelling.
2. My spelling's getting better.
3. Soon I'll be very good at spelling.
4. You've been trying hard, too.
5. I can't learn all the words in the dictionary.
6. I mustn't forget to practise.
7. Pablo couldn't spell contrariety.
8. Although he'd trained hard, he didn't win the marathon.
9. Oh no, it's started raining again!
10. Lulu couldn't wait for the holidays to come.
11. My uncle said he'd take me to Whistler.
12. I hope you're coming to my party.

TEST 81

1. impossible   2. uncommon
3. unimportant   4. displace, misplace
5. disrespect   6. unreliable
7. inexperienced   8. inconstant
9. disobedient   10. illiterate

TEST 82

1. correctness   2. movement
3. childhood, childless   4. childishness
5. socialism   6. leadership, leaderless
7. thickness   8. membership
9. fellowship   10. careful, careless

TEST 83

AMSTERDAM ATLANTA BOMBAY CAIRO DUBLIN ISTANBUL JERUSALEM LONDON MIAMI OSLO PARIS ROME SANTIAGO TORONTO WINNIPEG

TEST 84

a) GERMANY: it is a country, not a language b) MONKEY: you would not find it on a farm c) AUTHOR: this is not a member of the medical profession d) PLUM: it is not a vegetable but a fruit
e) DARK: it is not a colour
f) DARTS: you do not play this with a ball or balls
g) TREE: it is not a flower
h) ASIA: it is not a country but a continent i) OSTRICH: it is a bird but cannot fly
j) SOUL: all the others are fish. If this was spelled SOLE, however, it would also be a fish! k) BEER: it is alcoholic and the others are not
l) PLANE: it is the only type of transport listed that flies.

TEST 85

1. Yes 2. herbivore 3. 65 million years ago 4. b 5. They laid eggs
6. No, some were as small as chickens 7. Allosaurus, Velociraptor, T. rex 8. a herbivore 9. No

TEST 86

Saturday

TEST 87

1. Tuesday 2. No 3. 4   4. 1
5. noon 6. 6pm 7. 2pm

ENGLISH
ANSWERS

TEST 88
1. Sam travelled to Spain and met his friend Carlos there. 2. Ada has started learning Russian and hopes to go to Moscow next year. 3. We bought some food at IGA. 4. Anna is Italian and lives in Milan. 5. Switzerland borders France, Germany and Italy. 6. Mr. and Mrs. Singer live in Ottawa. 7. Can you speak Gujarati? 8. The Seine is a river in France. 9. My favourite singer is Avril Lavigne. 10. Princess Anne loves horseback riding.

TEST 89
1. Mark's favourite sport is lacrosse. 2. We are going shopping on Saturday. 3. It will be my birthday tomorrow. 4. Where would you like to go for your holiday? 5. Did you go to school today? 6. Ottawa is the capital of Canada. 7. Fiona takes her four dogs for a walk every day. 8. Do you think there are aliens on Mars? 9. We will be going fishing next weekend. 10. My favourite meal is hamburgers and fries.

TEST 90
ship, sea, passengers, journey, deck, waves, food, weather, Anton, West Indies, plane, trip, week.

TEST 91
l. play, day 2. toys, boys
3. eat, treat
4. holiday, away 5. cat, fat
6. ice cream, team
7. read, said

TEST 92
Alice was upset. She had misbehaved earlier in the day and her mother said she could not have her allowance. Her brother Bert, however, could have his allowance as he had behaved better. Alice spoke to him about it and he said that they could share his allowance. What a generous boy he was! Joy was just a little worried about going to her new school, but she knew that some of her friends were going there too. She would be able to see them at break times. They could all play together still, even if some of them were in a different class. Joy had a new uniform. It was grey and red. It was nicer than her previous uniform.

TEST 93
Julia's purse had been stolen. "I first noticed it was missing," she told the policeman, "when I got on the bus and found that I didn't have my fare." "How much money was there in your purse?" the policeman asked. "I can't remember," Julia replied. "It probably wasn't much. I spent most of it this morning buying John's birthday present. How lucky that I had already bought it!"

TEST 94
impatient, sunny, special, local, best, scrumptious, cool, home-made, sticky, marvellous, fantastic, wonderful

TAKE A BREAK
Story game
1. – B 2. – A 3. – D 4. – E
5. – H 6. – G 7. – F 8. – C
Crossword
Across: 1. address 3. lobe 4. tree
5. acorn 9. leek 10. pins 11. sleep
Down: 2. rob 3. leaves 6. rope
7. glass 8. knot

TEST 95
1. a ship 2. 6 days 3. yes 4. no
5. more than one thousand
6. Singapore 7. Thailand 8. Malacca
9. good 10. not known – he asked to remain anonymous

253

TEST 96
1. The fifth word should be spelled "mistake." 2. Amy – cheese and tomato/ Barbara – ham and lettuce/ Jemima – chicken salad/ Jessica – sardines and cucumber 3. If today is 1st January, and Francois's birthday was on December 31, then the day before yesterday he was still 10 and is now 11. He will be 12 on December 31 this year, and 13 on December 31 next year.

TEST 97
1. six thousand 2. a policeman 3. John Major 4. no 5. 13 6. Russia

TEST 98
whistled, walked, carried, swung, hurried, tripped, fell, hurt, rubbed, continued, was

TEST 99

Milly		John
Simon		Lucy
Andrew	OR	Sarah
Sarah		Andrew
Lucy		Simon
John		Milly

TEST 100
1. cold water
2. no
3. no
4. to the hospital
5. infection

TEST 101
quickly, easily, patiently, profusely, luckily, broadly

TEST 102
1. no 2. no 3. yes 4. a crisp apple 5. breakfast 6. in fruit and vegetables 7. because the body cannot store it 8. bread, pasta, eggs, soya protein, fruit, vegetables

TEST 103
bungalow, storey, chimney, conservatory, kitchen, dining, garage, burglar, scheme

TEST 104
1. Brian and Kevin
2. Ferncroft Road 3. a road with a blocked end 4. right 5. Mrs. Bolton 6. no 7. 45 minutes 8. right

TEST 105
1. c 2. c 3. b 4. c 5. c 6. b

TEST 106
1. SHY/TIMID
2. AVARICIOUS/GREEDY
3. PUTRID/ ROTTING
4. ESCALATE/ INCREASE
5. BIZARRE/ ODD
6. DONATION/ GIFT
7. ROTUND/ ROUND
8. FORLORN/ SAD
9. IMPETUOUS/ RASH
10. TEMPESTUOUS/ STORMY

RECORD SHEET

DATE	TEST	SCORE ✓ OR X	TIME

RECORD SHEET

DATE	TEST	SCORE ✓ OR X	TIME